How to get what you want

Unlock the magic of your mind and achieve your goals...

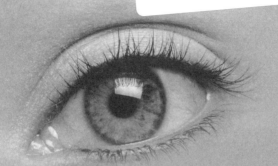

WITHDRAWN

Sandra **Cain** and
Michelle **Maxwell**

howto**books**

Published by How To Books Ltd,
3 Newtec Place, Magdalen Road,
Oxford OX4 1RE. United Kingdom.
Tel: (01865) 793806. Fax: (01865) 248780
email: info@howtobooks.co.uk
www.howtobooks.co.uk

British Library Cataloguing in Publication Data.
A catalogue record for this book is available from the British Library.

Produced for How To Books by Deer Park Productions, Tavistock
Cover design by Baseline Arts Ltd, Oxford
Typesetting and design by Sparks – www.sparks.co.uk
Printed and bound in Great Britain by Bell & Bain Ltd, Glasgow

NOTE: The material contained in this book is set out in good faith for general guidance and no liability can be accepted for loss or expense incurred as a result of relying in particular circumstances on statements made in this book. Laws and regulations are complex and liable to change, and readers should check the current position with the relevant authorities before making personal arrangements.

Contents

Preface

Congratulations! If you're reading this then you are someone who has already made a commitment to yourself. You are ready to move forward, explore what you want in your life and take action to get it. You are taking the time and energy to read, and even better, *do* the exercises that will help you find the key to *get what you want*. You are not alone, like many other people you are taking positive steps to find happiness and health.

Getting maximum results

A word of warning, if you want your life to stay the same as it always has been, this book is not for you. The information available to you in these pages can have a very powerful impact but *you have to use it*. Approach it as a partnership.

Research suggests adults retain:

- 10 percent of what they read
- 20 percent of what they hear
- 30 percent of what they see
- 50 percent of what they see and hear
- 70 percent of what they say
- 90 percent of what they say and do.

If you are really serious about making a difference in your life, you need to do more than just read this book. That will only give you a little nudge. If you want your life to be special, take off like a firework and light up the sky you will have to expend some energy and effort to make it happen. Doing the mind magic exercises and sharing the results with someone else will increase the power of this book. The more effort you put into *doing* as well as *reading* will greatly enhance the results. You will gain greater insights, increase your motivation, and flex those achievement muscles by being an active partner in the process. Discussing what you are doing with a sympathetic other will help you focus, commit and build support for what you want in your life.

Concentrate on doing the exercises as completely rather than as quickly as you can. Read them through first, then go back and *do* them. You are creating your future through the magic of your own mind. Just how wonderful could your life become?

> In order to change, you have to know what you want, know how to get it, and build a structure to support the changes you make.

In order to change through 'mind magic', you have to know what you want, know how to get it, and build a structure to support the changes you make. If the changes you make are in tune with your values, you will know without doubt that you are on the right path. Having a strong vision of yourself when you have achieved the changes you desire makes the changes easier and more compelling. That vision, based on what is really important to you, will help you plan the steps, build commitment and give you the confidence to go for what is right for you.

How to Get What You Want focuses on the way information is stored in our mind and body and in our nervous system. It is about recognising the influence of our language on how we store and express our understanding of ourselves and our world. It is about the unknown rules, values and beliefs that run in the background of our minds, regulating and informing what and who we are and how we live our life. It is about using the untapped magic of our minds to get what we want.

Mind magic as a framework for a life

Mind magic is one of the best and most effective ways to go beyond present, past and future limitations. It is a mind set resulting in action which helps people shape and direct their lives. Through unlocking the magic of your mind you can re-programme your mental coding of how you experience life to give yourself more options and choices. You can direct what you think, feel and do to produce optimum results for yourself. You can be the best that you can be. It may seem a very simple concept but the results it achieves are very powerful and profound. There is a world of potential which goes well beyond these pages – you are only getting a small taste of what is available. Many of the processes and results of unlocking the magic of the mind are best served by working with someone else one-to-one or in a workshop or training situation. The following chapters will enable you to take your first steps.

Mind magic – A way of looking at the world

Mind magic offers a tool bag of techniques and tools that help release your potential. Underpinning the use of the tools is a set of attitudes or presuppositions. The presuppositions are ways of understanding your experience that can help train your mind to be best friend and coach. These attitudes open possibilities for you to nurture and direct yourself to achieving your full potential.

1 Use the Magic of your Mind to Explore Changes

> 'You know what they say: There's only one constant in life, and that's change: and yet, why is it, I wonder, that the one thing that people can't abide above all others is change?'
>
> Quentin Bell
> The PR Business

When you know what you've got is not what you want, then some things will have to change – but change in the right direction. Yet the thought of change can evoke a variety of reactions. It seems to be the one thing we most hope for and desire and at the same time it can fill us with dread. Although the results can be exciting and fulfilling we may have to face fears and anxieties in the process. We have adapted to change in the past and we can do so in the future. Change is a learning process and through time it happens, whether we like it or not. We can choose our own path or be pushed on to one. Choosing the right path means looking at ourselves and finding out what excites and fulfils us. We can begin to passionately enjoy the life we are living. Overcoming obstacles and learning and growing from experience are part of life. Learning to enjoy and relish it can make it great fun.

Change is constant

We live in a world of uncertainty. Globalisation and new technological advances mean we need to be responsive and open to fast-moving shifts in our world. Established industries, professions and careers are closing down at a faster rate than ever before. Their replacements need new skills and new ways of being. Forty years with the same company is a thing of the past. We no longer live and die in the same place with our family around us. We have become a twenty-four hour, seven-day-a-week flexible society.

Many of our social values and constrictions have shifted, allowing us more choices and opportunities than we ever had before. The old restrictions of sex, class and race are receding. Women no longer stay at home and look after the family. They enjoy a greater amount of freedom than ever before. Working for pin money is an ancient myth. Women want to enjoy their work, make the best of their potential and lead a fulfilling life. Marriage and relationships have new shapes and individuals are defining for themselves how these partnerships will operate. The changing faces of work and relationships have repercussions for men too. They now have greater freedom to decide where they are going and what they want out of life. The old prescribed way of life is changing. The results of this are challenge, opportunity, insecurity and uncertainty.

Change can be challenging

We now have greater expectations of ourselves, our work, our partnerships and our lives. The desire for personal growth and fulfilment drives us to explore who we are and who we could be. It sounds wonderful and inspiring, so why are we all not jumping up and down with joy at the prospect of these amazing lives we could create for ourselves?

> The reality is, most people don't like change.

Making choices and changes in life can be perceived as very threatening. Most people don't like change. The thought of leaving what we know results in fears and anxieties. The hairs on the back of our neck can stand up; why – because change has that distinct smell of danger.

Making changes means leaving what we are familiar with and heading into something we might not feel safe with. The platforms or things that we have in place to make us feel comfortable and secure may be shaken.

For most of us the tendency is to want to hold on for dear life rather than go with the flow and reap the benefits. Even if we know what we want and even if it is available for us to have, our own reluctance to 'go for it' may be the only obstacle in our path. What stops us can be fear. The sort of fear that comes from anxiety, guilt or shame. The fear may not be grounded in reality but to the person who is experiencing it, it can be all too real.

The barriers – exploring anxiety, fear, guilt and shame

The barriers we erect are usually there to protect us. Unfortunately they can also stop us moving forward. One of the most common responses to change is anxiety. Anxiety can arise when we believe that the present or near future is threatening or even just unknown. On occasion anxiety can be helpful. It can make us consider different possibilities before action. It can motivate us to study for exams or research a new job offer before leaving our old one. On the other hand, it can also hold us back from doing what is right for us.

Anxiety really arises when we start to be open to the possibilities of something new happening. Anxiety goes with uncertainty, and with uncertainty is the space for something different and better than what we have already have. Why is that? Because if we always had certainty we would have what we already know, what we have had before. It is only with uncertainty that we can make way for something better. Unfortunately, anxiety can grow to monstrous proportions until it becomes overwhelming and damaging. As the perceptive French philosopher Montaigne once observed on behalf of many of us, *'My life has been full of terrible misfortunes, most of which never happened.'*

Here is what generates anxiety to paralysing proportions.

- When the fear of what could happen is exaggerated beyond the possibility of the situation.
- When we believe we could not cope with the situation.
- When we are unclear or confused about what is happening.
- When there is the possibility of violating an unquestioned belief or rule.

We may then suffer from internal conflict and not even know why!

The dangers of anxiety

Anxiety can lead us to catastrophise and to imagine the worst possible scenario. No wonder we would rather stay where we are than take action which may bring about our own private horror movie. Unfortunately, these terrifying images and stories we create in our heads often stay there, going round and round, building in intensity. We rarely share them with someone else, or listen to another voice that may give us a reality check and help us to imagine a different possible scenario. When we feel bad we rarely see a bright future or tell ourselves how good it will be. We are unlikely to make good decisions or perform at our best.

Case study

That was certainly true for Teresa, the mother of three young children. Although she had been very happy with her family life in the past, she had gradually become dissatisfied with her relationship with her husband. In the last few months they had bought a computer. Instead of it being good for the family, Jim was spending every moment at home online or playing with his new toy. He no longer helped with the children or spent time with Teresa. Although Teresa was very unhappy with the situation and was beginning to feel unsupported and more like a housekeeper than a wife, she could not bring herself to talk to Jim about it.

As far as Teresa was concerned, as soon as she mentioned it to Jim they would argue. He would storm out of the house, leave permanently, they would separate and then divorce. They would have to sell the house. She and the children would have to move home, probably to a horrible house in a bad area. The children would have to go to a child-minder and move schools while Teresa worked. She worried about what kind of work she would be able to do that could finance the family and how she would cope with the children on her own. Jim, of course, would remarry and have another family. Ultimately the children would be damaged by the

---

separation and grow to hate her. Maybe they would never want to get married themselves after experiencing their parents' failure. And of course Teresa would be alone for the rest of her life.

No wonder she was reluctant to talk to Jim if that was the outcome she foresaw. This outcome was right in front of her face with no room for any other possibility. It seems extreme to anyone on the outside but to Teresa this was a very real scenario and the only possible future she could see.

It was only when Teresa talked about her fears for the first time and actually heard herself speak aloud about the imagined outcome that she was able to recognise how unrealistic her fears were. She then started to see other possibilities. Past occasions came to mind when she had at first been reluctant to tackle a problem, but when she did she felt so much better about herself and the situation. Different outcomes from the one she had previously imagined came to mind. It still took courage for Teresa to talk to Jim, but it was easier for her once she realised she could confidently bring up the subject and it wouldn't automatically lead to the disaster she predicted.

Fear of not coping

Part of Teresa's fear was the anxiety of whether she could cope with the imagined consequences she had catastrophised in her nightmare. Even if the catastrophe had come true and Jim left home, would Teresa have been able to cope? Yes, she would and she might have learned that she was a lot stronger and more capable than she gave herself credit for. She might have come to value her independence and her new job. If Teresa had the confidence within herself to know she could handle the situation no matter how it turned out, she could have approached it without feeling helpless and scared.

Often our fear is the voice which tells us, *'No, you can't do that; what if you can't handle it?'* It can be a loud and powerful voice. A voice that has us hiding under the bed covers. Yet if we could use that loud and powerful voice to tell ourselves, *'Yes I can handle it, no matter what happens'*, we could come out from under the covers and take on the world, safe in the knowledge that we will be OK no matter what happens. Once we learn to trust ourselves, to build our confidence and draw on the resources we have within ourselves and other people we can begin to believe we can handle each step. We will cope with each day as it comes. We have handled much in the past and grown from it, so we can handle more in the future and grow further. We may even start to find joy, pleasure and a sense of achievement in coping with it.

Fear of failure

How many of us hold with this anonymous quote, *'I'm not a failure if I don't make it … I'm a success because I tried'* – probably the successful ones among us. It is usually only through failure that success comes. Failure is about learning what works and what doesn't, what produces the results or outcomes we set out to achieve.

> Failure is just feedback that tells us we may have to try something different.

Unfortunately, our expectations sometimes tell us we must be perfect all the time. Sometimes we have been hurt or put down when we were still learning. Often our unconscious tries to protect us and wants to stop us from being hurt again. Perhaps in the past we had tried something and it had not worked out the way we wanted it to. Maybe we put our hand up in class and didn't give the answer the teacher wanted. Perhaps we were laughed at or felt stupid. Maybe we tried a new sport like windsurfing and fell off, to the amusement of others. Or later in life when we tried something new and adventurous while still learning and perfecting it, others were saying, *'I told you so'*.

Our unconscious is truly on our side and it may decide that the best way to ensure we never fail is never to try anything in the first place. The pay-off is that we are safe. We may never be ridiculed or disappointed for failing but we still pay a very heavy price – we become victims of our own fears.

> Ultimately, the only failure is the failure to live your life fully, and that may be the biggest and most spectacular failure of them all.

Do I deserve it?

We may be afraid of succeeding because we believe at one level we don't deserve to. Think back to your family sayings (and see Chapter 5). Well, you may find that somewhere there is another loud and powerful voice telling you to 'know your place'. Many of the family sayings we have come across seem to be about keeping people in their place, keeping them from getting too big for their boots, or putting their head above the wall rather than recognising you are worthy of success because you are who you are. Instead, you may believe you have to be very smart or very hardworking or extra special to get what you want.

Instead of boosting their children's self-esteem and expectations, many parents believe it is safer to keep their children down and in their place in order to protect them. Indeed, not to let their natural exuberance and enthusiasm lead them astray. In order to stop them becoming too cocky, arrogant or selfish, children are sometimes encouraged to be grateful for any privilege they get.

Pride is mentioned as one of the deadly sins but you may consider that pride in yourself and your own worth is a primary requisite of a healthy person and a route to a healthy relationship. If you don't think you are worthy of love and a good life, how can you expect other people to think it? No one likes arrogance and egotism but that is a long way from appreciating who you are and recognising your abilities. If you doubt you deserve success, then you are sabotaging yourself. If you believe you are inadequate or not 'good enough' you may hold yourself back even more. If you do have any successes you may excuse them as luck, or you can tell yourself, 'phew, fooled them again.' Any explanation rather than admit to yourself that you deserve it.

And now that you are an adult and have some control and choice in your life you may wonder what would happen if your unconscious decided you did deserve everything you wanted. You may realise there are more useful ways of protecting yourself now.

Fear of success

What would happen to us if we became successful? We may even have ideas of what successful people are like and we may not want to end up like them. Would we stop being ourselves or would we become like those other successful people we know and don't like? It's a possibility, but is it a likely one?

- Would we become like those ruthless business people who exploit and abuse people?
- Would we have to work every hour of the day and shut out our family in the process?
- Would we lose all our friends if our circumstances changed?

Success can bring out characteristics and make demands on us that were not there before, but if you have balance and your success is consistent with your sense of yourself and your values, you will only become more of who you already are. No one can make you become anything you don't want to be, unless you let them. When you look at people who are successful but not good role models for you – observe and learn. Now you have a better idea of what you don't want in your successful life.

What comes after success?

For some people the journey itself is the pleasure and challenge. Once they reach their destination they get bored and want to move on again. Achieving their goal is the end of the fun rather than the beginning. If they are unable to set themselves a new destination or have a new direction in mind they panic. Without another dream, they are looking at a big blank screen and that is a recipe for depression.

> Sometimes being successful can challenge every belief about yourself.

Always have another step in your fulfilment ladder, and when you reach the top of one ladder you can always start at the bottom of another one.

Case study

Michael and his two partners met at university and had gone on to form a business partnership developing software for the insurance industry. Their business always ticked over, surviving but never really breaking through to become very successful. Similar companies to theirs had been doing very well and there appeared to be no real reason why they could not do the same.

Then Michael started to ask himself, what was stopping them from making the business grow? In their university days they had been part of quite a political group and were very much into social justice and changing the world. Even though they themselves had become businessmen they did not want to become 'one of them', an exploiter (in their eyes). For them exploiting others was against their values and their sense of who they were.

Once they realised they had made the very large generalisation that all business owners exploit, when in fact there were plenty of examples of business people who were wonderful employers and who made a valuable contribution to their community and environment, Michael and his partners discussed ways to have both success and their valued social conscience. They removed their blinkered and outmoded way of thinking and found ways to make their business grow in a way that was in total harmony with their values and their sense of selves.

Fear of upsetting the apple-cart

Who else would your success affect? Each of us is part of a system. We are members of a family or a group of friends. That group or system is part of a larger system – our community. Our community is part of the larger community of our culture and our country.

When we make decisions and changes in our lives it affects other people. A change in one part of the system has repercussions for the rest of the system. When Abby went back to work full time, her decision had repercussions for the rest of her family. Initially they all tried to ignore the change and continue as before, but eventually the family system negotiated and adjusted to a more equitable way of running their home.

What happens to the mum whose child goes off to school? What happens to the parents when their children leave home and mum and dad are left alone in the house together? What happens to the husband who doesn't want his wife to get a job and be too independent in case she doesn't need him any more? What happens to the wife who doesn't want her husband to become too successful in case she cannot fit in and be part of his new life? What happens to the family dynamics when the 'average' one becomes more successful than the 'bright' one? What happens if one of a work team gets promoted over their friends?

The repercussions of change

Each change has repercussions for everyone. Sometimes we may think it's easier to stay where we are rather than rock the boat. We all have our own place in each system and when we change that place the whole system gets realigned. In that period of realignment we may lose the certainty and predictability we have been used to. And uncertainty and unpredictability can lead people to hang on to what they know for dear life. Sometimes the rest of the system can try to keep the balance of what was there before.

We are part of a pattern; when we change, the pattern changes. It is not unknown for a marriage to break down after the alcoholic or drug-addicted partner has become clean. Their long-suffering partner no longer has the role of martyr to play. The co-dependent relationship that kept them together is no longer supported by their partner's behaviour.

The husband who sees himself as the breadwinner and decision-maker in the family may not want his position to change if his wife becomes independent. He may do everything in his power to keep the status quo. You may not be the only one who is apprehensive about uncertainty and change.

Try it for yourself

What would happen if you changed?

- If you are someone who is always there for other people, what would happen if you said 'No' for once?

- If you are someone who is always nice, could you be not nice on occasion?
- If you are always diplomatic, never wanting to offend, what would happen if you were open and honest about your feelings?
- If you are someone who is always efficient and organised, what would happen if one day you threw your hands up and said, 'I've had enough, I can't cope'?
- If you are someone who is a rescuer, could you occasionally ignore someone in trouble?
- If you are someone who is always supportive, could you ask for support on occasion?
- If you depended on someone to take care of you, what would happen if you decided to become independent?
- Who else would be affected by your changing? Could they cope with it? If they couldn't cope with it, could you cope with them not coping with it?
- Is their possible discomfort enough to stop you doing what you want?
- Is it OK for you to do what you want even though others might disapprove of or be hurt by it?

You may find that some of these questions have provoked some thought and perhaps a little trepidation. Don't worry – this means you are really beginning to challenge your comfort zone. You are beginning to discover your trouble spots. When you begin to discover what stops you and what you are afraid of, then you can start to find ways of dealing with your self-imposed limitations.

Stepping outside our comfort zones

When we face the fear of change we can begin to rob fear of its power. We each have a comfort zone – areas that we operate in easily. However, when we start to think of stepping outside our comfort zone we get stopped. Some of us may be fearful of stepping outside our comfort zone because we imagine that we don't deserve a better and more fruitful way of life. Our limited place of being is all we know, and even if we are offered an opportunity to stretch ourselves literally and metaphorically we are often nervous of making that change. Like animals in a zoo we adapt to the size of our cages. Often these cages are self-imposed, and we act as though we have constraints when in reality we have none but our own fear and insecurity. Like the tiger caged in a small enclosure who, when offered a new, much larger enclosure still paces up and down nervously, unable and too fearful to explore his new boundaries.

The dichotomy is that each of us has expanded our comfort zones through time. There are things that are normal parts of our lives that we now take for granted but they may have been intimidating to us before we had the courage to do them.

Try it now

Relax and get comfortable. Let your shoulders drop and your breathing flow. Remember a time when you were apprehensive or uncomfortable about doing something but you did it anyway. Take yourself back to that time and fully experience what you saw, what you felt and what you heard when you did it. Remember how good it felt when you had expanded your comfort zone and knew you had accomplished something. You learned to step outside your comfort zone because you wanted to or had to. The fear was probably still present when you did it but you went ahead anyway. You took action despite the fear.

Fear may always be with you but you can learn to rule it rather than let it rule you. You may even come to value it.

If you continue to step outside of your inhibiting personal framework, your comfort zone will increase until there are no limits left at all.

Fear: False Evidence Appearing Real

Fear only comes when we perceive a challenge or when we perceive a risk. Without fear there is only certainty. Fear is a signal of growth, of stepping outside of what we know. You can learn to welcome fear, or at least look at it with new eyes. You can teach fear to sing a new song – a song of excitement, learning and achievement. Fear can become a friend, a friend who only wants to protect you. Like most friends it only has your best interests at heart. It may be working on old information, it may not realise how much you have learned and that you are now able to cope with new situations. It may be based on old beliefs or false evidence. It may be willing to reach a compromise. If you can assure fear that you are taking it seriously and not ignoring its warnings, it can help you achieve what you want.

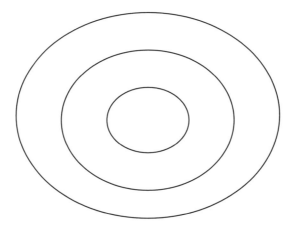

Figure 1   Your comfort zone expands each time you do something new.

Fear is a signal of growth, of stepping outside of what we know.

Dealing with guilt

Guilt can also hold us back. Guilt comes from a sense of responsibility for someone else's well-being. It can be helpful for signalling us when we have violated our values or sense of self. It can remind us to take others into account and regulate our behaviour, but it can also be damaging when:

- we *always* put the needs of others before our own;
- it comes from breaking a rule rather than a genuine response; and
- we don't or can't take action to remedy the situation.

Case study

Joan is a wonderful woman who spends most of her time helping other people, elderly neighbours, her mother and her family. She also works as a special needs assistant for children with learning disabilities. She has a very busy life and is always running around trying to get everything accomplished. Her life is made more difficult by the fact that she is unable to drive. What stops her from learning to drive is the fear that one day she might just keep on driving and never come back.

Joan knows she always puts others before herself, and at times resents it but she believes that is what a *'good'* woman does. And if she is not a *'good'* woman, then what is she? What compounds it for Joan is that she knows she *'should'* also take time for herself but she still can't bring herself to do it. She is caught in a Catch 22 situation – feeling bad for wanting to do something different and feeling bad for not doing it. The thought of making any kind of change just brings more guilt.

Rules, obligation and necessity

Joan suffers from a terrible affliction called *'rules, obligation and necessity'*. One of the quickest ways to discover if you or someone you know is afflicted with this unhappy and cruel disease is to listen to what they say. Their language is the first symptom; it is also part of the disease and surprisingly, the means of their cure. If their conversation is littered with *'should'*, *'must'*, *'ought to'*, *'have to'*, *'need to'*, then this person is in need of serious help. Suffering from *'rules, obligation and necessity'* robs you of choice, fun and pleasure. When you are doing something because you should or have to, you are doing something under pressure. You are robbing yourself of options and wearing the martyr's gown. The disease can come from many sources, usually buried in the past but the cure is in your own hands, or should we say in your own head.

When you decide to do something because you choose to rather than have to, you become motivated and energised. You are coming from a place of freedom and power – not victimisation and pain.

Experience it for yourself

Make a list of five things you know you should do. Here are a few prompts to get you thinking:

- lose weight
- get fit
- clear out the garage/attic/wardrobe
- network
- apply for a new job
- phone an old friend or family member
- take time for yourself.

Once you have made your list, take each item one at a time and change the '*I should…*', to '*I wish to…*', then '*I ought to…*', and continue down the list. As you listen to yourself, pay exquisite attention to how you feel with each sentence.

Consider how motivated you are to do each task when you change how you say it:

- I should…
- I wish…
- I ought to…
- I'd like to…
- I have to…
- I need to…
- I must…
- I want to…
- I can…
- I will…
- I'm going to…
- I am…

Language changes experience

Now that you have done that with each item on your list, do you notice how the language you use changes your experience? The language of
'rules, obligation and necessity' is best avoided if you want to remain motivated and energised. Now that you have introduced some choices, which
ones are you actually going to do?

It may be interesting to go back to the ones you decided not to do and
ask the question, *'Who says I should?'* You may discover from where you
originally caught the disease.

Whenever you are making judgements about something or someone,
ask yourself – *'Who says?'*

When Joan did this exercise she discovered she had quite a few *'rules'*
she was carrying around with her. She uncovered her belief that doing
what she wanted, in her terms, meant *'being selfish is bad'*. By asking *'Who
says?'* she was able to decide whether the belief applied at that moment
and in those circumstances. The *'selfish is bad'* belief may have had some
merits for her when choosing what television channel to watch with her
sister and brother as a child but it certainly was not helpful for her to
live her life as an adult with that as a governing rule. Joan still wanted
to take care of her friends and family but now she had more choice. She
experienced more joy, energy and happiness in what she did for others
because she was caring through freedom and choice rather than obligation and necessity, which hinged on an old belief or rule she had adopted
as a child. The part that was telling her she 'should' take time for herself
was the adult Joan crying out for nurturing and attention for herself.
After changing the *'should'* to *'could'*, Joan decided to make it *'I will take
time for myself.'*

Dealing with shame

Another powerful emotional inhibitor to change, is shame. Shame can
come from the deeply-held belief that *'I have no right to exist'*. It may be
present in a variety of ways for different people, such as *'I am not good
enough'*, *'I am stupid'* or *'I am bad or worthless'*. The intensity of feeling,
the feeling of shame, the fear of being discovered can hold us back from
putting ourselves in positions where we may be exposed. It is painful
enough for us to 'know' it, without letting everyone else know about it
too. No matter how bizarre or ridiculous these notions may be to others,

they are a powerful force to the individuals who believe it about themselves. This lack of confidence and self-doubt can be the biggest barrier to any sort of fulfilling life. Unfortunately these deeply-held beliefs and misconceptions can rule and regulate our lives, even if we are not consciously aware of them. They can permeate every action and intention.

The same belief can have different manifestations for different people

The belief 'I am stupid' can drive one person to dedicate themselves to great academic success, getting degree after degree to prove to themselves they are anything but stupid. In some ways it may help them to achieve success in other people's eyes. But for the individual themselves, they feel they have no choice. They are driven by the need to prove themselves. For someone else, it may mean they avoid situations where they get exposed – not taking a demanding job or a promotion, not speaking out at meetings, not going out with 'smart' people. We rob ourselves of choice.

Yet most people seem to feel inadequate when they look and listen to others. And many of us invest a lot of energy in trying to hide it. The way to combat shame is to learn self-acceptance and be open to a sense of connection with others. When you see yourself and others as they truly are, you can breathe a sigh of relief knowing you are just like everyone else. You are the only you there is, you cannot be compared with any other you.

> Accepting yourself will be the most powerful step forward you can ever make.

The price of self-doubt

Unfortunately, anxiety, guilt and shame can compound each other and act as a powerful emotional force that can immobilise us. Self-doubt can be crippling. Even if we take action we can sometimes pay a heavy price. While we are resisting change we tend to waste time and energy worrying, which can be very disruptive and stressful.

Fortunately not all of these effects will apply as a result of stress and worry, but even one or two effects are enough to leave you feeling unresourceful. Making decisions and taking action becomes even more difficult.

When you worry, you:

- feel overwhelmed and out of control
- feel unconfident
- hype yourself up, stopping yourself from sleeping and relaxing
- make yourself tense and weary
- give yourself headaches and stomach upsets
- get confused and apprehensive
- stop trusting yourself and look outside for guidance
- focus on yourself and your problems
- become preoccupied, can't concentrate and drop in efficiency
- focus on what is wrong or could go wrong in your life.

Going beyond limitations by unlocking the magic of your mind

The magic of our minds is not 'out there' somewhere. It is in our head. So often it is not the external world we live in that stops us, it is the internal one. Most barriers to getting what you want can be overcome – if you are flexible. If you are 55 and a woman, no matter what you do you will never play football for England in the World Cup. Some things we can't change. But there are many things we can change if we really commit ourselves. The challenge is to know when we can't change things and knowing when we can. Even if we find there are some things we can't change we can often ask ourselves, *'What would having this get me? What would playing for England mean to me?'* It might mean being famous, earning lots of money, being successful or proving a point. How else could you achieve those things? Would writing a book, starting a business or winning a marathon bring you what you want?

Often the first answer to 'What do you want?' is 'winning the lottery'. When we go past that and ask 'What would that mean for you?' what we hear is 'no more worries. I'd be able to help my family. I could do what I want. I could go travelling.' The money itself is not very important – it is what it can do for you that is. Surprisingly, when you start to talk about 'what it does for me', you can look at it from a new angle and start to find ways to satisfy your desires right now without winning the lottery. When it comes to things you can control you can find ways to fulfil your desires straightaway.

Look at Tim's Fulfilment Ladder (Figure 2) and see for yourself how it is possible to find ways to get what you want right now. Tim found that winning the lottery, his daydream when he got fed up, would allow him to learn and grow. He soon realised that he could find ways to learn and grow immediately without that winning ticket.

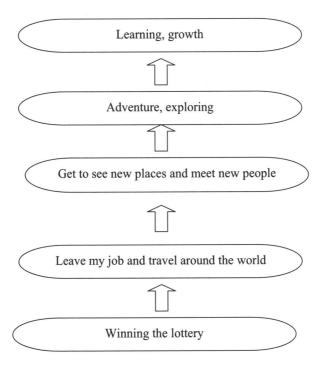

Figure 2   The fulfilment ladder

Try it for yourself

Work through your own fulfilment ladder:
1 Start at the bottom box, fill in what you would like in your life.
2 Ask yourself:
   a) What would this do for me?
   b) What would this bring me?
   c) What would this mean for me?

Fill in the second box with this answer.

3 Keep on working your way through the boxes, until you know you are satisfied or have gone as far as you want. You may find you reach some qualities or values that are very important to you. When you discover these you may find you can find ways to satisfy them right now.

The first step in changing what is going on *out there* is changing what is going on *inside*. When you unlock the magic of your mind to look at things with new eyes and hear new interpretations you are opening yourself up to doing things differently and can achieve so much more.

Change is about learning

'Let me assert my firm belief that the only thing we have to fear is fear itself.'

F.D. Roosevelt

Change is primarily about learning. Learning how to adapt and handle new situations, skills, attitudes, beliefs and behaviours. Learning that our fears are not always real, learning we can handle change no matter what, and learning we are important and deserve the best life we can have. We all suffer from uncertainty when we face the unknown. Some people let it spur them on, feel excited and challenged, others get stopped and feel helpless and small. Yet we can all learn to challenge our limiting beliefs and learn to look at the positive possibilities change can bring.

The only way to get through the fear is to take action.

Fear will not go away on its own; it goes away when you show yourself you can overcome it. And overcoming it is easier and less painful in the long run than staying stuck in helplessness and smallness. For those who see change as an exciting challenge and a great learning experience, the world is at their feet. For the rest of us who are less enthusiastic, change can be a daunting prospect. Yet it is a prospect that has always been with us. We have learned to deal with it in the past, we can learn to do so again in the here and now, and in the future.

Change is a process

So change is always with us. Whether we like it or not – change happens. Being alive means change. We start off as newborn babies and grow into maturing adults. At each stage of our development we face new challenges, new situations and new life stages. We change schools, friends, homes, jobs, and relationships. Sometimes we have to adapt to losing friends, jobs, homes, family and relationships. Other times we gain them. We cannot escape change. In our technological age, change is the one constant we have. We live longer and expect more from our lives than previous generations ever dreamed of. We face social upheaval in our family, work and life. Look at how much you and your world has changed since you were five years old. Change is a constant process. How we deal with it makes the difference.

> Taking action despite the fear is easier than staying stuck in helplessness and smallness.

Valuing life's lessons

Often when we look back at some of the events in our life we start to appreciate that even the most traumatic times of change brought with them a great deal of benefit. For some reason it seems that we grow more from bad times than good. It is only with the perspective of time that we appreciate what we have gained. It is only afterwards we can see the silver lining of the life's lessons we have experienced.

Try it for yourself

Draw a horizontal line across a page to represent your life.
For each positive event in your life draw a vertical line up the page
from your life line. Represent the negative events with a vertical
line below. Make the line correspond in length with the importance
or benefit of the event in your life. Do the exercise twice:

- for how the event seemed at the time
- and from today's perspective looking back.

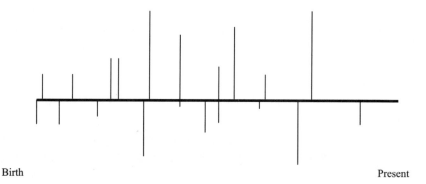

Birth   Present

Figure 3   Your timeline

How much have you benefited from even the most difficult of times?
You might find a corresponding 'up' line for every 'down' line. All those
things you thought were mistakes and failures were in fact lessons to be
learned – feedback enabling you to know what you do and don't want in
your life.

The perspective of time

What would it have been like with the benefit of hindsight? How would
your experience change if you were able to start with all the lessons you
learned after the event and all the knowledge you have now? What would
it be like if you could float back in time to that younger you, and give
the younger you the benefit, experience and guidance of what you know
now? The younger you probably deserves your love and compassion.

How would you be different if you had been able to be there as your own guardian angel?

You may find you would have done things differently. You may be more compassionate and forgiving to yourself. You always did the best you could with what you had at the time. Now you are taking stock of where you are and where you want to be, you are in control of your life and making choices. You are a survivor, someone with very good coping skills. Now you can really start to fulfil your potential.

As you work your way through the chapters you will discover what you want from your life and learn how using 'mind magic' can help you break through the barriers that are holding you back.

Summary

Change is a constant part of our world and our own individual lives. For many of us change is frightening, but for others it is a challenging, rewarding and liberating experience. As individuals we can build many barriers around us that inhibit change. Most of these barriers are based on fear or guilt. Fear of failure or even fear of success can stop many of us from moving forward. It takes courage to step outside of our comfort zones and go beyond our self-imposed limitations – but it can be done. Understanding that change is a process, learning to combat fear of change and valuing life's lessons are the first steps towards creating a more fulfilling life.

- Change can be intimidating and challenging.
- Change is a constant process that is always with us.
- Anxiety, fear, guilt and shame are all self-imposed barriers to having a great life.
- Fear of failure or even fear of success may inhibit change.
- You are part of a system, therefore any changes you make can have profound repercussions for others.
- Your comfort zone continually expands the more you step outside it.
- The language we use structures our thought processes and changes our experiences.
- Change is about learning how to adapt to new situations, new attitudes, beliefs and behaviours.

Every change brings positive benefits in the long run.

2 Use the Magic of your Mind to Deal with Change

> 'Where change is desired ... entered upon willingly and achieved with sensitivity, it can be ... very rewarding.'
>
> William Stewart

We all deal with change in different ways. Through time we tend to develop our own personal strategies. We can...

- ignore it and pretend it's not happening
- resist and insist our way is best
- accept it, once persuaded
- be excited by the thought of something new
- come alive and thrive on it.

We may use different strategies in different contexts. Someone who thrives on change in some areas of their life may be hard pushed to accept it in other areas.

Case study

Jenny is a prime example. She is a very attractive, assertive businesswoman in her forties who is always looking for ways to be innovative and more successful in her business and her own personal development. One of her personal goals is to learn a new skill every year. She actively initiates change and thrives on it. Yet her marriage is in trouble. To everyone around her the evidence suggests her husband is having an affair but Jenny refuses to acknowledge it. This change in the status quo of their relationship is too threatening for Jenny to face. Her fear of being abandoned (the only outcome she can imagine) keeps her from addressing the problem and from creating a potentially better relationship with her husband.

Jenny is not alone. We all have some areas in our life were we make changes easily, even if it is only moving our furniture around, changing our hair colour or our car. In other areas we like to keep things the way they have always been. The person who changes their job every two years may go on holiday to the same place they have been going to for the last ten years.

Case study

Phil, an analyst programmer with a large financial institution, has been with the same company since leaving university fifteen years ago. Yet in that time he has been divorced twice and moved home six times. As soon as he settles in one place, he starts thinking about finding somewhere new and better. For Phil, moving home is exciting, an investment for the future and an achievement. Moving jobs is not. Although he is frustrated in the position he is in, his fear of failure keeps him stuck in the same old unsatisfying job he has outgrown.

Responding to change

Sometimes we can go through many responses depending on the situation. The change curve shown in Figure 4, developed from the work of Elizabeth Kubler-Ross, identifies the stages we may go through when undergoing change.

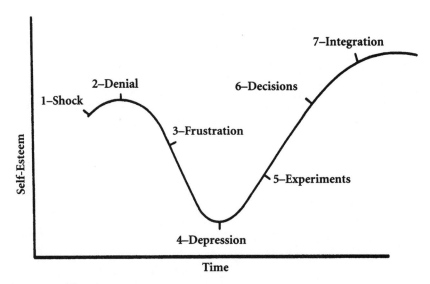

Figure 4 The change curve

Stage 1   *'It can't be true'* – Shock, surprise and disbelief in response to
the event, situation or change.

Stage 2   *'Ignore it and it will go away'* – Denial and reassuring ourselves
that it is not really happening. 'The ostrich stage' when we stick
our head in the sand and hope the problem will go away.

Stage 3   *'Why me'* – Recognition of what is happening. Our self-esteem
starts to suffer and we experience anger, frustration and unhappiness at the change. 'Life is not fair.' Still fighting it, maybe
resentful, blaming others. At this point we can turn on others:
'It's all their fault!

Stage 4   *'I've had enough'* – Crisis point: experiencing apathy and depression, our confidence and self-esteem can sink to rock bottom. In extreme cases this can lead to illness and suicide, but it
can also be the point at which we really recognise that we need
help.

Stage 5   *'I can't stand it anymore, I need to do something'* – We begin to
try new things. Somewhere inside us the motivation to move
out of depression kicks in and we try to move forward. We may
seek help to pick ourselves up and deal with it.

Stage 6   *'Maybe I could get to like this; it may just work'* – We begin to
accept the change, to become hopeful about the future. We

decide what does and doesn't work and start to feel good about it and ourselves.

Stage 7   *'Yes, this is the new me'* – Confidence is at a high as we begin to make changes in our life. We start a new way of being.

Many people can get stuck in different phases, skip stages or circle back and forth between stages. We can also vary in the time it takes us to go through the process.

Case study

When Anne came to one of our workshops she explained what had brought her there. She was thinking about changing her job again, a job she had been doing for only a few months. (Anne was at stage 5; she was ready to try something else). She liked the people she worked with and thought she could really do well at her job, if she was allowed to get on with it. Unfortunately Anne had got well and truly fed up with it. (Anne had been in crisis; she had been very down and lethargic about it, stage 4.) Ralph, her boss, was always trying out new ideas and procedures. Initially she thought it might be the fact that he was training her for the position that had brought about this constant review of how things were done. (Anne was in denial, hoping things would get better, stage 2). He might be just looking at the job with new eyes. But as time went on her unhappiness grew (frustration and beginnings of depression, stage 3) as she realised that this was normal behaviour from Ralph.

Anne had always considered herself to be a competent person but she was beginning to doubt herself. Since she never got on top of any change before it changed again she began to doubt her ability to do the job. She started to lose confidence in herself. Fortunately a good friend could see what was happening and persuaded Anne to come and take the opportunity of a 'mind magic' seminar in order to find a direction for herself. Since it was Anne's first experience of a self-development workshop she was slightly apprehensive and very curious about who else would be there.

▶

As the workshop progressed she became more reassured and glad she had come along. As other people explained what they wanted from the weekend she realised she was not alone. Many of the other participants were there because they wanted a direction for their lives or they wanted to find a way to make or confirm a decision. She was also relieved to find out that others were looking for motivation and confidence to make changes in their lives. When she saw the change model she had a eureka! moment! She became excited as she recognised where she and Ralph were on the change curve. He was one of those people who liked initiating change, just for the pleasure and excitement of it. He liked experimenting with different ideas but never gave them a chance to work. It was a great relief to Anne to see she was 'normal'. Somehow she thought she was the only person who had trouble adapting to new ideas every few days. Just knowing that she was exhibiting a 'normal' reaction to change was enough to restore her confidence in herself. She was reassured and feeling better about herself and her job already.

And it got better for Anne as the day progressed. Working through the exercises, Anne began to discover her values. Love, friendship, laughter, adventure and success were the most important things she wanted in her life. These were the things that would bring her happiness and contentment.

She had further surprises in store. When she had designed a life that would be in keeping with her values and her sense of self, she knew she wanted to start her own business and be her own boss. She decided for the following year she would plan, gather information and start to put things into place for becoming self-employed. She realised she could learn a lot from Ralph, and the skills she already had could be enhanced by working with him. It was also important to her not to leave her job without talking to Ralph and sounding out a way to compromise. Her idea of herself was of someone who saw things through and did not quit. Leaving without getting on top of the job would not fit in with Anne's sense of 'who' she was. She wanted to find a way to work things out with Ralph.

She thought about showing him the change curve model but was a bit apprehensive as to how he would react, but when Anne put herself in Ralph's shoes she realised what it was like for Ralph.

He had started the company in the last few years and was frustrated that the business was not growing as he felt it should (Ralph, stage 3). He was doing everything he could to make it work better, more efficiently. He enjoyed the challenge of trying out new ideas and of directing his business (Ralph, stage 5).

Unfortunately he had not realised how depressing it was for his staff to contend with goalposts that were constantly shifting (Anne, stage 4). When Anne understood this she felt she could approach Ralph and explain how his actions were affecting her. Instead of improving his business he could be losing good staff (as he had in the past). Anne appreciated that if she pointed out to Ralph how important it was to build his business and keep his staff, he could be persuaded to give each idea a chance to work and not change things just for the sake of change.

Anne's goal for the week following the workshop was to show Ralph the change curve (Anne, stage 5). At our follow-up session Anne explained she had had the meeting with Ralph and had shared with him what had happened for her at the workshop. She explained the change curve to him and he recognised that he had been shunting back and forth between frustration (Ralph, stage 3) and experimentation (Ralph, stage 5) without ever giving any new idea time to work (stages 6 and 7). Now he is aware of his pattern he is giving a new idea or procedure a chance to see if it works before rushing in with another new change (Ralph, stage 6).

Anne reported that she and the rest of his staff are also a lot happier at their job (stage 7) now they are not subjected to constantly moving goalposts. And as an extra bonus, they are a lot more open in their communication with each other. Ralph has become a mentor to Anne, helping her to avoid the pitfalls of starting her own business and encouraging her with new ideas. His excitement at change is being put to good use by helping Anne research a new business while letting her get on happily with the job he is paying her to do.

Isn't it great to know you are not alone; that there is a normal human response to change? If you are beating yourself up for not immediately embracing the thought of turning your world upside down, stop now. You're only human.

Abby's journey

Can you identify the stages Abby went through?

- Abby took 12 months to get her life back on an even keel. She had gone back to work full-time after being at home looking after her two children. She continued to be responsible for most of the housework as before.
- Needless to say, she became very tired and overworked. At first she did not realise she needed to stop being 'supermum'.
- But eventually she became so stressed. Her life seemed to be a never-ending juggling act, never having time for herself or for having fun with the family.
- It all got on top of her and she became depressed.
- She decided she had to make some changes, for her own sanity if nothing else.
- She realised she could not and did not want to continue taking care of the house and family all by herself, especially now the children were teenagers. Abby decided she needed to learn to say 'No' sometimes. The family had got used to her always taking care of them but circumstances were different now. Abby called a family meeting and negotiated a work schedule that allowed the rest of the family to help out.
- Eventually Abby established a routine that worked for her and the rest of the family. It wasn't always a smooth transition; there were times when Abby had to restrain herself from picking up after the family or doing the jobs they 'forgot' to do, but eventually it paid off. In time the family learned to adapt and play a bigger part in taking care of themselves. Abby was more able to cope and consequently felt much happier. She felt proud of herself for drawing up and sticking to her boundaries. It also taught the rest of the family a lot about co-operating and being responsible for themselves. When Abby's children left home they were well equipped to take care of themselves.

Abby's situation is not unique. Many mums going back to work face exactly the same problem and get exhausted and stressed out before they insist on changes to the domestic responsibilities.

A smart lady once said, 'If you usually wait until your back is against the wall before you make a change why not save yourself a lot of time and trouble. As soon as you know what to do – do it!' There may be some validity in that.

Discover how you react to change

Do you recognise any relationship between your response to change and the change curve? If you are dealing with something at the moment, can you see which stage you are at right now?

If you are a person who likes things to be the same as they have always been or thinks more about the past, or likes to avoid things, it is likely that you will get stuck feeling depressed, and may tend to cycle back to the denial stage. People with this pattern can stay stuck in unhappy situations for years and years before they take any action to change the situation. They may be trying to avoid the pain of the unknown, accepting the devil they know rather than the devil they don't. Unfortunately avoidance can often make the problems worse and can increase the difficulty of facing them.

> The sooner any potential problem or opportunity for change is identified and acknowledged, the sooner you can start to tackle it and the more effective you are likely to be.

You can get on with living your life fully instead of ducking and diving away from what you fear is coming. Yet if you look back at your timeline exercise you will find that the process of change can eventually bring a great deal of benefit. Facing difficulties or change is rarely as alarming in reality compared with how it is in your imagination. Avoiding the situation only allows it to grow in magnitude in our imagination.

> You are not alone; many people find making changes a big
> challenge.

Most people are daunted by the last three stages: trying out new things, deciding what works for them and then making them part of their life. It can take quite a while before they move from denial, frustration and depression into actively finding ways to enjoy the changes in their life. You are not alone; many people find making changes a big challenge.

Discover your approach to change

Look at your normal pattern for dealing with change. It may vary according to the circumstances or context. When you are aware of your normal response you can watch out for the danger points for yourself. When you know where you usually get stuck you can be prepared and help yourself along to the next stage.

Find out for yourself

Think of a time in the past when you had to deal with change over which you had no control. How did you respond when:

- There was an imposed change at work?
- There was an imposed change at home?
- There was an imposed change in an important relationship?

Do you notice a general pattern for dealing with change that is imposed on you? Is there a difference between contexts? How do you handle imposed change at work compared with that in the home or relationships?

Often there is a difference between how we handle imposed change and change we have some control over. Ralph liked initiating change. Part of his enjoyment was being in control and directing his business and his life. He responded very differently when change was imposed on him. Rather than welcome the change with open arms he would get very angry and try to fight it. When he failed to get things the way he wanted them he would get depressed. How did you respond when:

- There was a change at work you had some control over?
- There was a change at home you had some control over?
- There was a change in an important relationship you had some control over?

What is your general pattern for responding to change you have some control over? Again, is there a difference between contexts?

If you have some insight into the way you handle change it makes it easier to understand where you get challenged. You can then choose to move forward or choose to stay stuck.

However, we may not always be the best judges of our own behaviour. We may criticise ourselves harshly or we may suffer from selective memory, believing we sailed through a dramatic change without batting an eyelid when in fact we either denied the change or got stuck in one of the stages. Often it helps to get a different perspective, especially from people we trust to be honest with us.

Try it now

Ask two people who know you well, one in a personal and the other in a professional capacity, how they think you deal with change. They may see your responses in a different light than you do.

Managing imposed change

You may have noticed that you respond to change that has been imposed upon you in a different way to change that you choose for yourself. In some ways being in control can make it easier. You feel as though you have some freedom and choice.

What we need to be happy

Control and predictability seem to be basic human desires. We often want to feel that we have some control over our environment and our destiny to feel safe. This control of self and sometimes others allows us a sense of power in our life. Yet each of us varies in the amount of control we require.

We are also directed and motivated in finding ways to:

- ensure our basic safety and security
- fulfil our need for affection
- experience a sense of belonging or connection to others
- express who we are.

Survival needs such as food and shelter involve our physical well-being. We also have a requirement for relationships, affection, love and esteem. The urge to belong, to feel connected to other human beings and to identify with them is common to us all. We also need to let ourselves and the world know who we are, through what we do and what we say. We all share the desire to express who we are.

Individual differences

The way these needs motivate us varies according to individuals and circumstances. If someone has a high need for connection, it does not necessarily mean they have a high need for affection. Often individuals will join groups or want to be invited along by people they don't particularly like just to feel part of something. Similarly, someone who has a strong need for affection may not want to be part of a large circle of people but may be satisfied with a close relationship with one or two people.

Acknowledging our needs

As we live our life we find ways to satisfy these needs. If they are satisfied they diminish in significance, but if there is the threat that they will go unfulfilled then we can start to panic. There is a big difference between being hungry and knowing you will eat in an hour, compared with being hungry and not knowing when and where the next meal is coming from. The need for food is universal; everyone needs to eat in order to stay alive. But it may be less common for us to acknowledge our other requirements. We may fear that others will judge us, think us weak, needy or selfish. Yet everyone has needs and motivations. It's part of being human.

When our needs are threatened

Unfortunately, there are times when we really value someone or something and we lose what we treasure; especially when what we value has fulfilled one or all of our needs. It may be a person, a job, a lifestyle or anything that is important to us. In these circumstances imposed change can be very painful indeed.

As well as the loss itself we can lose our sense of power and control and feel battered by life. We may lose our sense of belonging or our source of affection and trust. As well as anger and frustration, we may feel lonely and alienated. Often the acknowledgement of our powerlessness in the face of circumstances can be as painful as the event itself. We do not have to suffer a bereavement to understand grief; the anger, pain, confusion and upset can accompany any kind of loss. All we can do is adapt to the new circumstances but like any kind of change, it is how we respond to it that prolongs the pain.

If we start to move forward and look for ways to adapt we may still feel the loss but in some ways we can benefit from it. The loss can alert us to what is really important to us. Once we recognise what the qualities were of the things we valued, we can look for ways to bring more of those qualities into our life in the future. When we recognise our needs we can find ways to fulfil them.

Case study

When Mike's wife left him, he was devastated. Although he knew his marriage was in trouble he had been in 'the ostrich stage', ignoring it and it hoping it would sort itself out. When he realised his wife was gone he went through many of the stages recognisable from the change curve. At first there was shock, then

▶

disbelief, then as he came to accept that she wasn't coming back he became very angry and blaming towards her. He spent many days and nights in a deep depression.

When he really started to think about his relationship he began to differentiate what was good and bad about it. The more he identified what was good about his relationship the more he was able to start bringing the valued qualities back into his life. He had enjoyed the closeness and friendship that had previously been in his marriage. Although he was not ready to get into another romantic relationship, he started to talk more with a couple of his friends. He created those missed qualities in his friendships and acknowledged how important they would be in any future relationships. He started to fulfil his need for affection.

He also discovered how important being a father was to him. Although he had previously taken his children for granted he was now determined to appreciate them and be as close to them as he could be. Being part of a family had given him a sense of connection to others. He looked for ways to bring laughter and fun back into his life, something else he had enjoyed about his family life. It had given him a place to be playful, to express that part of himself. And the more he took action to bring the things he appreciated and needed into his life, the more he felt as though he was directing his life again.

Although his divorce was a very painful experience Mike recognised what was important to him and to any future relationship. He took responsibility for his part in his marriage breakdown and was determined to learn from the experience.

When the decision is made for us

Other times we may be quite happy with an imposed change. It can be easier for us if the change is thrust upon us, such as when a partner in an unhappy relationship makes the decision and leaves first or when we are made redundant from a job we disliked. We are absolved from making the decision. If things do not turn out as well as we planned we can blame circumstances or often other people for what happens rather than ourselves. When a change is imposed we don't have to face the prospect of making a wrong decision, of being responsible. We were 'forced' into it. Strangely enough if circumstances force us to make a change that proves to be very successful we are usually more than happy to take credit for the outcome ourselves. Some of us only like to take responsibility for our actions when we look like heroes. When we don't look so good we like to blame the situation or others.

Choosing to change

> 'To make the growth choice instead of the fear choice a dozen times a day is to move a dozen times a day towards self-actualisation.'
>
> Abraham Maslow

While choosing to change may be exciting and give us control over our lives it can also create internal struggle. Taking full personal responsibility can be very difficult because we are choosing to leave what we know as safe and familiar, no matter how painful it may be. We may have some self-interest in staying where we are. There is always a payoff for preserving the status quo, even if it is only being safe. Sometimes the fear of what we don't know can keep us stuck. How many times have you thought about making a change but have been held back by the thought *'Am I doing the right thing?'* At some level we are asking ourselves *'What could I lose?'* No matter how difficult our situation is, maybe if we are staying stuck in it we are getting some payoff from it.

So we are not only dealing with the process of change and all that it involves, but also the taking of responsibility for making a choice that may not be the right one. A choice we might regret. Yet those changes we make for ourselves can be very empowering. A major difference in our approach to change can come from how much we take control of it. It then becomes our choice of what to leave behind, what to take with us and what is ultimately right for us.

Taking responsibility for the changes you make

The price you pay for making changes is that you stop being a victim. While on some level we don't like to think of ourselves as victims, there is also great comfort in blaming someone else or blaming our circumstances for where and what we are. It is a great let-out clause for what is wrong with our life – but it costs us. We are like a ship at sea battered by tides and winds instead of steering our own course. We rarely get to go where we want to go.

You have a choice in how you feel, think and act

It may not always seem like it but you do have choice. You have choice in relation to yourself, in relation to others and to your circumstances. You can navigate your own course. You have choice in how you feel, think and act. You own your feelings, you own your thinking and you own your actions. They don't own you. It takes effort and practice to be successful in managing yourself but it can be done, even in the most horrendous of circumstances.

Viktor Frankl in his inspirational book *Man's Search for Meaning* tells the story of the Nazi concentration camps where a few powerful individuals chose to rise above their barbaric conditions. When nothing of their life was left except the *'last human freedom'*, the ability to *'choose one's attitude in a given set of circumstances'*, these people turned their personal tragedies into triumphs of the human spirit. Instead of becoming victims they became victors in spirit, not just for themselves but for others too.

Another wonderful example is Stephen Hawking, perhaps the best-known scientist of our generation. At the age of twenty-one he was diagnosed with amyotrophic lateral sclerosis (ALS), a disease which attacks parts of the brain needed to produce voluntary motor function. He was given two years to live. Now, nearing 60 years old, he can look back on a career that includes being the youngest scientist to become a Fellow of the Royal Society, followed later by his appointment as Lucasian Professor of Mathematics at Cambridge. He was awarded the CBE by the Queen and in 1989 became a Companion of Honour. His book *A Brief History of Time*, (Bantam, 1995) held a place on the best-seller list for over four and a half years and he himself is easily recognisable from his television series *Stephen Hawking's Universe* and his cameo appearance on *Star Trek: The Next Generation*.

In an article in *Frontiers* he states that instead of being devastated by his illness, it spurred him on. 'Before the illness set in I was bored with life', he explains. 'When one's expectations are reduced to zero, one really appreciates everything that one does have.' Stephen Hawking's determination to live his life to the full, regardless of his situation, provides inspiration to us all. He chose to make full use of every resource at his disposal. He chose not to be a victim.

> The price you pay for making changes is that you stop being a victim.

Taking responsibility is making the decision to be in charge of your life. It means you have to decide what you want, then find ways to get it. You may think that everything would be wonderful if your partner or your boss or your circumstances changed. If only you had a magic wand to make it all better. But the only person you can change is yourself. When you take charge of your life, you can make it go places.

If you think and act as though you are responsible for everything in your life (even if it is not true) then you can change everything. If you think or act as though someone else is responsible then you have to wait until they change, and that may never happen.

Why change is easier when you know what you want

Going places is simpler and more successful when you have a destination in mind. Making a change is easier when it is based on what you want, rather than what you don't want. If you are considering a change because you are not satisfied with what you have without deciding what you want instead, you are handicapping yourself. You are backing away from the present instead of walking into the future. And walking forward is much easier than walking backwards, especially when it is into the unknown. When you want to go somewhere it is wise to look ahead and choose a direction.

Deciding what you want means you are taking responsibility. It means you have thought it through and have made a declaration of intent. You have something to focus on and it concentrates your efforts in that direction. It allows you to be enthusiastic, plan, build commitment and know when you have arrived. What you want can be a great prize worth striving for. Knowing what you want gives you power and courage and a reason to go for it.

If you picture a future that is bright and colourful, full of wonderful enticing things, it will draw you forward. It will motivate you to move forward through apprehension and barriers. If you know what you want, you will have a much better chance of getting it.

> When you want to go somewhere it is wise to look ahead and choose a direction.

Summary

We all deal with change in different ways. Some of us ignore it and hope it will go away, others thrive on it. Sometimes we go through many different responses or stages depending on the situation, or can travel back and forth between varying stages. Many of us handle change over which we have some degree of control in a different way to change which has been imposed upon us. However, change can be very difficult to adapt to when our individual needs such as security or love and affection are threatened. It is much easier when we know what we want from life when we take responsibility for change, and recognise where our direction is taking us.

- We all respond to change in different ways.
- It's *normal* for change to affect your confidence; in the end it can boost it.
- Our pattern for dealing with change varies according to the circumstances or context.
- Imposed change is often harder to handle than changes we have some control over.
- Taking responsibility is making the decision to be in charge of our life.

Change is easier when we have a destination in mind.

3 Use the Magic of your Mind to Understand your Values

This chapter is designed to help you discover what is important to you and what you really want and need in your life to be happy. For most of us there has been a time when we planned, worked hard and achieved exactly what we were after, only to find what we were after didn't actually bring the benefits or happiness we expected. Other times we are so unsure about making a decision that we never actually get round to making it. Sometimes we bumble along, never really knowing where we are going or when we have arrived. No more! When you use 'mind magic' to get in touch with who you are and what your values are you harness inspiration. You get filled with purpose and passion. You know where you are going and you get there fast. Once you identify your values you can use them to create a life that is empowering, exciting and fulfilling. One that is right for you!

Knowing what is right for you

Our future is a blank sheet of paper just waiting to be written on. If we are going to write a life story it may as well be an exciting and fulfilling one. In order to design that great future and make the necessary changes, we first need to know what we want and decide which is the right path for us to follow.

Often we have a good idea of where we would like to go, but other things get in the way. We seem to have conflicting demands or interests. We may be waiting for the right thing to appear, but waiting for the right thing may stop us from doing anything. We can get bogged down and confused. We wanted to go out and save the world but we watched TV instead. Our priorities can conflict or get muddled. We know we want something better, different, but we don't know what. We know what we should do, but is it really going to make us happy? Is it worth the effort?

Knowing yourself

The only person who can know what is right for you, is you. The only person who can know if it is worth the effort is you. The only person who knows what they want to change is you. You have to know where you are *now* before you can step forward. If you want to make changes in your life it is necessary to make the internal changes before making the external ones. You need to make decisions before you go into action. You need to change your way of thinking in order to change the results you have been getting.

If you are someone who has been involved with self-development you may already have a good idea of who you are, what motivates you and turns you on. If this is the first time you have read this type of book many of the exercises and ideas may require you to look at yourself with fresh eyes. You may feel unsettled and discover aspects of yourself that you had not recognised before. Imagine yourself as a pioneer who is exploring new territory. You are learning and growing.

> You need to change your way of thinking in order to change the results you have been getting.

When Mike's marriage split up he began to look at himself and evaluate his life. It was only then that he recognised what his values were and how important they were to his happiness. He had never taken the time to really look at his life before and discover who he was and what was important to him.

Like Mike, knowing your values tells you what you want to do, what you don't want to do, what you want in your life and what you don't want in your life. Your values are a guide to what you are likely to enjoy doing or what you feel strongly about.

> Your values are very closely linked to what motivates you.

They fulfil your needs and are the things that can drive you. Values can change over time as you grow and learn and your circumstances change. The values which may have been important to you as a young person leaving school or university and starting out in life may be very different to your values when you have a family or when you retire.

Case study

Paul had a very successful and well-paid job as an IT contractor. He and his wife were used to him spending a lot of time working away from home. There were compensations; they had a lovely home and when Paul wasn't working they could go away on holiday to exotic locations. They had a wonderful lifestyle that they were happy with.

Things changed dramatically for Paul and his wife when his daughter was born. He hated leaving his family when he went back to work. The great lifestyle and fantastic holidays no longer had the same appeal. The small bundle of noise and nonsense had a much greater pull than two weeks in the Maldives. Suddenly Paul's values changed – his family became more important to him. He and his wife sat down and talked about it. Between them they decided family life was a priority for them. Paul found himself a job nearer home. He took a large drop in salary but coming home every night and weekend was more important to him.

Why values can light the way

For many people there is a spiritual element to their values – a spiritual link between their values and some sort of higher purpose. When they live life according to their values they are following a spiritual direction finder. For others, values give a sense of what is right for them.

Many of your beliefs are based on your values. Beliefs and values are highly connected. Values are things that are very important to you. They are principles, standards or qualities considered worthwhile or desirable. There are no right or wrong values, only *your* values.

Robert Dilts, a communication guru, suggests people operate on six levels of influence:

- *Spirituality*: Is there something greater than me? Who or what else is there?
- *Identify*: Who am I? What is my personal mission?
- *Beliefs and values*: What and why is it important to me?
- *Capabilities*: How do I make it happen? What skills and abilities do I have?
- *Behaviours or actions*: What do I do?
- *Environment*: When and where do I do it?

Each level influences the other. When each level is aligned and in harmony, the individual has balance and congruity. When there is inconsistency or conflict between the levels then the result is stress and internal sabotage. Think of how you react to politicians who preach family values yet are discovered in compromising positions. That same politician will be causing himself a great deal of pain, stress and inner turmoil if he does indeed believe that his behaviour is *'wrong'*.

That is why your values, which may appear abstract and reserved only for the big decisions in life, can be very much part of the everyday choices you make, even the little ones. Very often, values lie behind *'I can't ...'.* What is really meant is *'I don't want to. It does not fit in with my values and beliefs, with who I am.'*

Your values can influence:

- where and how you live
- the skills you learn
- how you behave

- the relationships you have
- the career you choose
- the way you respond to events
- the priorities you place on relationships and activities
- how you spend your money
- how you divide your time
- how you relate to the rest of the world
- how you think and feel about yourself
- what you hope to achieve.

There are no right or wrong values, only your values.

Whose values are they?

Often we have adopted other people's values without taking the time to discover what our own values are. What your parents, friends or peers want and need in their life may not necessarily be right for you.

When we talk of values, we may think we are talking about the same thing but each person has their own way of fulfilling a value. We all want to be happy but what makes one person happy may make another dissatisfied. Many of us still want the same things – a *good* job, a *good* relationship, a *good* life, but it is our own individual values that guide us in knowing what *good* is.

Just as values vary among individuals, so do ways of fulfilling them.

For one person a *good* job may be a job that is secure, high status, financially well rewarded with an excellent career track. For someone else it may be the opportunity to work in a creative team, with the freedom to explore and generate new ideas. For someone else a *good* job may be making a contribution, helping people and showing compassion.

Excitement for one person may be riding their motorbike; for another it is changing their hairstyle, or buying a new book, or having an affair.

Security for one person may be having money and not having to worry about paying the bills. For someone else *security* may be the ability to trust they will be able to handle anything no matter what happens. *Nurturing* for you may mean taking care of people by cooking dinner or washing clothes. For someone else *nurturing* may mean allowing their children to do it for themselves so they know they will be able to manage when they are on their own. Or *nurturing* may mean hiring someone else to take care of things at home so you can be happy and energetic enough to spend quality time with your family. Some people, mistakenly, never apply *nurturing* to themselves.

Identifying behaviours that fulfil values

Once we have identified what values are important to us we can start to find other behaviours to fulfil them. If someone loves going out horse riding and galloping their horse over a field, the value this fulfils may be *exhilaration*. Once they have identified the values concerned they may find other activities or behaviours that can satisfy them. They may enjoy those same qualities performing on stage, windsurfing, riding a motorbike or jet skiing.

Finding different ways to bring your personal values into your life increases your ability to feel happy and satisfied. It makes it easier to adapt to life's changing circumstances. It allows you to be flexible and initiate change yourself, knowing you can find ways to bring about what you want in your life.

Values in all areas of your life

Values can relate to the four different areas of your life:

- world
- career
- relationships
- yourself.

All these areas overlap and there are times when they may be in conflict with each other. There are also times when the same values are constant through each area.

In our workshop situations, participants are often surprised and delighted at the things they learn that are important to them. For us, it is such a pleasure to see someone who has reached deep inside and discovered that the things they really hold dear and value are not the things they first thought of. It is so easy to spot someone who has discovered their values – they radiate with happiness, they stand taller and seem more alive and vibrant.

Living life through your values means living life as fully as you can. It is incredibly worthwhile getting in touch with your values. You will be uplifted and motivated by them and you will begin to access within yourself a potential and sense of self and worth that is very powerful.

Discover your values

Values give you direction. They provide very useful information for gaining a life that fulfils, satisfies and excites you. These exercises may also confirm that there are things you don't want in your life. If you are going to create a great life, make sure it is one that meets the values you *'do'* have and not the ones you *'should'* have.

In this section you begin to choose for yourself the values you would like to live by. This is an important and self-affirming choice to make. And it is one that can have profound affects on how you move into your future. Keep a record in your notebook. You will be delighted with what you find out in these discovery sessions and it will help you now and in the future.

Discover for yourself

Savouring special moments

Take some time to review the last five years and note down some of the highlights and achievements. They don't all have to be winning the Nobel Peace Prize. It could be something as simple as planting something new in the garden or getting a project completed on time. It could even be a day at the beach with the family. Think of good days, things you felt happy about, memories

▶

and moments that sparkle. It would be helpful to find things from each area of your life, such as successes in your career and in your relationships. Think about what was happening in the world and yourself as an individual at that time.

When you have finished finding these special moments and achievements take the time to go back and fully experience them. Re-live that experience. Savour and enjoy them again and notice what you saw, what you felt and what you heard.

We will come back to this exercise later.

Now you have looked at the past and celebrated it a little, we shall move on to the future. Let's step outside time and reality and enjoy a flight of fancy.

What would you do if you had a 'Magic Wand'?

For the next five minutes use your imagination and write down anything and everything you would want to do, be, have, create, give, share, discover, see, feel, hear, make, in your life over the next year if you had a magic wand.

You can create materialistic things or emotional things. You can think on a spiritual level, a physical level, a social level, a mental level, anything – think as big as you can. What is the point of a magic wand if you don't use it? What would really inspire you? Would you want world peace and a perfect body? Perhaps a red, top-of-the-range soft-top, a great singing voice and social justice. Go for it! Let your imagination soar. Put the realist to one side and become the dreamer. Take your feet off the ground and let yourself rise up into the clouds. Right now all you have to do is let yourself enjoy the sensation of playfulness and fun as you, the dreamer, wave your magic wand.

When you have finished waving your magic wand, and your feet are back on the ground, consider what is important to you about the things or experiences you have created.

Again, we will come back to this exercise at a later stage.

What it means to me

Now you are starting to recognise what is important to you. You may already know what values are very significant for you. You may already be realising what you want more of in your life. Just as a prompt, the list that follows has come from some of the participants of our workshops. These are the principles, standards or qualities the participants considered worthwhile or desirable. You will probably have your own to add. You may find some of the listed values surprising, liberating or enlightening.

As you read the list you will notice that some values will appeal more that others. Take note of the ones that particularly feel significant for you. Trust yourself – some of them will just feel right or ring a bell for you. Some may sparkle and shine compared with others. You will know what is right for you!

Values are very personal. There are no right or wrong values, only your values.

Exploring values

Here are some values others have mentioned as values they want in their life. Use them as a prompt and add your own.

Some worthwhile or desirable values in each life area

World	Career	Relationships	Personal
Peace	Ambition	Closeness	Self-acceptance
Harmony	Fun	Sharing	Giving love
Respect	Fulfilment	Identity	Self-love
Equality	Excitement	Love	Excitement
Freedom	Personal development	Shared consciousness	Personal development
Stability	Success	Companionship	Freedom
Health	Contribution	Appreciation	Harmony
Wisdom	Love	Freedom	Self-esteem
Understanding	Pride	Fun	Confidence
Laughter	Challenge	Acceptance	Health
Balance	Security	Friendship	Balance
Acceptance	Pleasure	Comfort	Challenge
Love	Self-esteem	Support	Change
Nurturing	Confidence	Security	Wisdom
Connection	Achievement	Warmth	Creativity

World	Career	Relationships	Personal
Sharing	Freedom	Contribution	Understanding
Appreciation	Independence	Stability	Security
Forgiveness	Power	Laughter	Fun
Compassion	Social interaction	Tender loving care	Peace
Trust	Passion	Flexibility	Honesty
Honesty	Self-expression	Pleasure	Fulfilment
	Growth	Passion	Integrity
	Flexibility	Adventure	Choice
	Honesty	Trust	Compassion
		Self-expression	Awareness
		Sensuality	Passion
		Harmony	Trust
		Safety	Safety
		Beauty	Adventure
			Orgasms
			Family
			Self-expression
			Beauty
			Sensuality
			Exploration
			Nature

Combinations of values

You may find one value encompasses other values as component parts. For one person, *self-acceptance* may also mean *confidence, warmth* and *love*. For another *confidence* may also mean *self-acceptance, laughter* and *ambition*. Again there are no right and wrong combinations, only your personal combinations.

Discover for yourself

When you've been living your values

Go back to your past highlights and achievements and for each event note which values you were fulfilling at the time.

Values you'd like to live by

Do the same for the life you created with your magic wand. Which were the values you were creating in your life?

Values for giving direction

Like a general commanding an army our conscious mind directs our unconscious. Can you imagine how confused and disorganised an army would be if their battle orders were a list of things not to do? *'Don't go back into the sea, don't stay where you are, don't stand up in open view, don't run out of ammunition.'* Wouldn't the troops be more effective if they were given orders that directed them towards achieving a specific task? How about, *'Land onshore, advance up the beach as far as you can, carry enough ammunition and supplies with you. If you meet enemy fire, dig in and defend yourself until you have a chance of successfully advancing.'* Which plan do you think would be more likely to succeed? Which plan would be more likely to motivate and organise the troops? You've got it – the one that focuses and directs the action. What to do rather than what not to do.

Give yourself a greater chance of success. Give yourself a direction and state what you want in the positive. You do know what you want but you may have been used to focusing on what you don't want. If you focus on what you don't want you really cut your chances of what you do want. All you will do is find lots more things you don't want.

Remember to walk into the future instead of backing away from the past. Instead of saying what you don't want, find a way of saying what you do want. If you don't want to feel stupid or insecure you may want to feel confident or valued. If you don't want loneliness what do you want instead? Maybe closeness, sharing, love, shared consciousness, companionship, friendship. If you want to stop criticising or being hard on yourself, what do you want instead? Do you want confidence, self-esteem, self-love, and self-acceptance?

If you can only come up with things you don't want, keep on asking yourself, *'What do I want instead?'* Only you will know what you want.

> Walk purposefully into the future instead of backing away from the past.

Similarly, you are the one reading and doing the exercises in this book. The only person, at this moment, you can influence to change is yourself. If you want something like winning the lottery, or your boss, your partner or your kids to change, ask yourself what that would do for you. What would you gain by having that happen? You may find you have a desire for a value to be fulfilled but are not ready to satisfy it for yourself.

Values for balancing your life

We may have different values for each area of our life and we may find they compete. If you really want a world free of pollution but work in a company that is damaging the environment, you are bound to find you suffer from an internal conflict at one point. Similarly, if spending time with your family is very important to you, but being successful in your career means putting in a lot of time away from home, you have a hard balancing act to achieve. When you are clear about what is important to you in each area of your life and what is important to you overall you are in a much better position to keep your life stress-free and balanced. And a lot less likely to lose the things you value.

Your values can be the best time management tool you will ever need. Instead of filling your time with the urgent but unimportant stuff, you can start to prioritise and do what will bring you the best in happiness. That doesn't mean we can do away with the mundane, it just means the mundane does not become our life.

When you tap into your values you will find you become energised and excited. You will be very much more satisfied with your life and your decisions. You will soar. If your values are not being met, you are likely to become dissatisfied, disheartened or bitter. When you are living to someone else's values, you are living to how you 'should' and that is pressure and drudgery. Living how you 'could' live is much more light-hearted and fun, and you deserve that.

Even if you are sure you know what your values are, run through the exercise anyway. It never hurts to reaffirm those matters that you know are important for you.

Discovering your values

1 To help you identify your values for the **world** ask yourself:
   - What do I want in the world?
   - What do I want to feel about the world?
   - How would I like the world to be?
   Identify at least seven world values. Which of these are most important? Place them in a hierarchical order.

2 To help you identify your **career** values ask yourself:
   - What do I want from my work?
   - What is important to me about my career?
   - How do I want to feel about my occupation?
   - What would the perfect job be like?
   Identify at least seven career values. Which of these are most important? Place them in a hierarchical order.

3 To help you identify your **relationship** values ask yourself:
   - What do I want from a relationship?
   - How do I want to feel about my relationship?
   - What is important to me about my relationships?
   - What would the perfect relationship be like?
   Identify at least seven relationship values. Which of these are most important? Place them in a hierarchical order.

4 To help you identify your **personal** values ask yourself:
   - What do I want from my life?
   - What is important to me about my life?
   - How do I want to feel about my life?
   Which values are most important? Place them in a hierarchical order.

Many of us live as though we are immortal. We put things off until the right time. But the right time may never come. If you thought you only had a short while left to do everything you wanted to do, do you think you would continue your life the way it is at the moment?

Try it now

Imagine you had only '1 month to live'

- What would you do?
- Where would you go?
- Who would you see?
- What would you say?
- What are the things you would really appreciate in your last few days?
- What would you do that you had never done before?
- What would you like to enjoy again?
- What would bring you the greatest happiness?

Look at your plans. What are the values you have chosen in your last month? You may find they surprise you.

Values summary

Now look back at all the values you have identified in this chapter. Which ones do you recognise as essential to you being happy and fulfilled? You may notice the same value keeps on appearing in each list, which could be an indication of its significance to you. It is now time to focus on the most powerful ones for you.

Note the 5 values *you must have in your life* in hierarchical order. Start with the most important. Ask yourself:

1 When did I know I didn't have it?
2 When did I know I did?

When were you happiest, when didn't you or when did you have that value present in your life? Continue for each value. Identify when you did and didn't have it. When you recognise what you were doing, how you were behaving, who you were being when your values were met, it is an invaluable guide for yourself in the future.

If you want the life you create from now on to be happy and fulfilled, having these values in it will make a difference.

Summary

You are the only person who can know what is right for you. Your values give you a sense of what is *right for you*. They are the principles, standards or qualities you consider worthwhile or desirable. They are personal to you and there are no right or wrong values – only your own individual values. It is important to realise that values are subjective and can mean different things to different people. Recognising the values by which you want to live your life can have a profound effect on how you move forward into the future. They can be seen as a guiding light that shines on the right path for you.

- The only person who can know what is right for you – is you.
- Values are principles, standards or qualities we consider worthwhile.
- Many of our beliefs are based on our values.
- There are no right or wrong values.
- Inherited values may no longer have meaning for us
- When we live in tune with our values we are more likely to have balance in our life.

Values can light our path in life.

4 Unlock your Values and Get what you Want

> 'Identify what you need to do in the present to get what you want in the future.'
>
> Cain and Maxwell

Now you have identified your values, let's use them to design your future and visualise what it will be like to be living life according to your values. Use this exercise to identify what you really want, what your purpose is and give yourself a direction that fits in with your sense of who you are.

By visualising your life as it could be when you are in balance, your values are fulfilled and you are living your life in accordance with your life's purpose. You are then motivated and inspired. The way forward becomes clear and the changes you need to make are obvious and made easier. You can give yourself a future that will fill you with joy and pleasure now. You will begin to live in the present – excited and compelled by a great future, instead of attached to your past. You can take the beneficial learning experiences of the past and use them to nurture yourself in the here and now and in the future.

The benefits of hindsight

Remember your timeline exercise in Chapter 1 (Figure 3) where you looked at the lessons from the past? When we look back at the past we often have a different perspective on it. How wonderful it would have been to have given ourselves the benefit of hindsight *before* rather than after the event. How much easier it would have been for us to go through an experience fortified with the knowledge we would have gained through time. How different is your perspective on the completed task – compared with before it? Would that hindsight have been valuable if you had had it when you started out? There is a way it can be so.

Reorganising time

Most of us organise our sense of time spatially. If you watch someone who uses their hands a lot when they are talking, you may notice them waving or pointing in the direction of future or past depending on what they are talking about. The lovely thing is, they know at an unconscious level how they organise time but they are not aware of it consciously.

Try it now

- To get a sense of where your past is, point to the memory of something that happened yesterday, last week, last year.
- Now that you have an idea of where your past is, point to where your future is. It will probably be in the opposite direction to the past.

Many people keep their past behind them and their future out in front of them. However, others arrange time in different ways. Some have a sense of time as a spiral rather than a straight line. Others imagine time is out in front of them arranged as a horseshoe curve with the past out to the left, the present close and in front of them and the future out to the right. Again there are no right or wrong ways of arranging time – just your way. No matter how you arrange it you do have an understanding of where it belongs for you.

At many of our workshops, one of the most important discoveries for participants is the extent to which we are all similar and also all different. When we ask the group to point to their past and then their future, most people know where it is. They may not know why they know, but they know that they know. Everyone has a place for the past and a place for the future. And everyone can have them in a different place.

Case study

Once we are aware of it we can start to do some useful things with it. When we talked about the potential for hindsight at one of our workshops, one of the participants named Maria immediately said, *'Oh I wish I could have that now.'* Since Sandra was holding the magic wand we passed around for the earlier exercise she put it to use. 'OK, if that is what you want let's give it to you.'

Maria explained she had started a new career as a driving instructor and was due to sit her advanced driving exam the following week. As the exam got nearer she was becoming more and more anxious. She was dreading the exam, to the extent that she had begun to consider dropping out rather than go through with it.

'So Maria, you are anxious about your driving exam next week; would you like to come up here and we will do something about that?'

'Yeh, I would, thank you, Sandra. I'm really dreading it. I'm getting so stressed by it I'm thinking about not doing it. But I have spent so much on it already and I can't just drop out.'

'Well, let's take care of that. Maria can you point to your future?' (Maria laughs and points to her right). 'Great, can you imagine a line on the floor that represents your life?'

Again Maria laughs and nods. This is the first time she has done anything as strange as imagining time as a line on the floor but since fun and laughter are important values for her she is willing to go along with it. Especially as we reassure her it works.

'Where on your timeline is the present?'

Maria points to a spot on the floor. Sandra drops a paper on the spot to mark the present and asks, 'How will you know you have passed the driving test?'

Maria thinks for a moment and explains, 'The examiner will tell me and give me a pass paper with any comments on it.'

'Point to the moment just after you have passed your exam. Your examiner has told you have passed and you've got your pass paper to prove it.'

Maria points to the spot, Sandra marks the spot with a magazine, then Maria adds *'but I'm not sure I'm going to pass it.'*

'We might as well assume you will pass it. It's just as easy to assume you will rather than won't do well.' (Remember, tell your brain what you do want.)

Sandra turns to the group and addresses everyone. 'We all have a tendency to imagine the worst. Practically every one of us goes for the worst possible scenario when we think about the possibilities of what could happen. We have this great big private movie screen in our head, and what do we show on it? Horror movies! Disasters!' (Most people in this and other seminars, nod their head in agreement. You are not the only one who imagines the worst.)

'Just as an experiment, let's show an alternative type of movie. One where everything goes right for you. A movie where you behave with style and confidence. You do whatever you want easily and effortlessly. Would you like to try that? How about a movie of yourself being successful and happy for a change. Maria, show yourself a movie of what it will be like when you know you have passed and have been given your pass paper. Listen to the examiner telling you you've passed. See yourself being given the pass paper. Go further, you might want to imagine yourself telling other people the good news, you could see yourself celebrating your success. Enjoy it, try it on for size, see how it feels. You are now well on your way to becoming a driving instructor'.

Maria smiles and looks up at her own private cinema screen in her head. After a few seconds she looks back at Sandra and nods her head. *'That was much better, I might even do the exam now and pass.'*

'OK, you've seen yourself do it and you're happy with that, are you?'

Maria nods. She does looks happy and pleased with herself.

Sandra points to the future spot on Maria's timeline. 'Take that movie image of yourself and put it on your timeline just after the moment you knew you had passed your test. Imagine yourself having passed your exam. You have heard the examiner tell you the good news, you have passed. Now you have that important piece of paper in your hand, you're happy and celebrating. Make it a big, bright exciting image, so enticing that it draws you in. Then go and step into that moment.'

▶

Maria steps into the magazine that marks the future spot. She straightens her shoulders and her face lights up.

Sandra gives her a bit more encouragement to fully experience her achievement. 'Soak up those good feelings. Really enjoy how wonderful you are, how good you feel.'

Maria breathes deeply for a moment or two and opens her eyes. Sandra asks, 'What is it like?'

Maria beams, 'It's great. I'm over the moon. It just went so well. I feel like a great big weight has been lifted off my shoulders.'

'What did you learn from the experience?'

Maria shakes her head and smiles slightly. 'All that worry was for nothing; what a waste of time and energy.'

'Where has all the worry and anxiety gone?'

Maria shrugs her shoulders and replies, 'I don't know, but it has definitely gone.'

As Sandra points to the present spot on the timeline she tells Maria, 'Take that new understanding back to the present'.

Maria comes off her timeline, walks back to the present mark and stands straight facing her future.

Everyone else in the group can see how confident she is by looking at her. Sandra asks, 'What is it like now?'

Maria is bursting with enthusiasm. 'Amazing, I just want to get on with it. I feel motivated, excited about it. I can't believe how much I want to do it now. Thank you. This stuff is powerful. Hindsight is just so amazing.'

When we spoke to Maria a couple of weeks later, she had in fact passed her advanced driving test. The exercise had made a big difference to her approach to the test. She told us she felt more confident and assured behind the wheel and that she concentrated on what she was doing instead of telling herself how badly she was feeling. When she sat the test she was able to let her true driving abilities show. She had already used the exercise for her next challenge, the theoretical test, and she had used the process to help her daughter prepare for a school dance recital.

Turning anxiety into confidence

This exercise can be particularly useful if you are worried about something in the future. With hindsight you can turn that anxiety into confidence. Depending on what the event is you may find yourself motivated and excited at the prospect of what is to come. You may be excited and looking forward to it or sometimes you may even discover this is something you do not want to do.

This can be very useful if you are someone who metaphorically *jumps off cliffs*. Some risks are fun, others are just stupid. No matter what happens, visualising this timeline technique will give you access to more information and perhaps a different perspective. You can only gain by that.

Experimenting with hindsight

1 Take a moment and think of something you have to or want to do in the future. Something you may be a little nervous or apprehensive about. Maybe something you are intimidated by. It could be a visit to the dentist, your appraisal with the boss, a big project coming up.

2 Once you have chosen something imagine a line on the floor that represents your life. Put the past in one direction where it belongs and place your future out in front of you. Mark where your present is on the line with a paper or magazine. Mark, again with a paper or magazine, a spot in the future when the event is over and you are pleased with the outcome.

3 Imagine you have a large cinema screen in front of you. On the screen there is a movie of your life. You have just completed something you were doubtful about. See and hear yourself being pleased with how you've done now you have completed the event. Watch yourself being happy with the outcome. Imagine what it will be like for you when you are celebrating and congratulating yourself. What would you look like to other people? What kind of things would you be saying? How would it feel?

4 Once you have a strong image of yourself, put that image on your timeline in the future. Step into that image of the successful you. Let the good moment bathe over you. You are the screen hero. See it through your own eyes. Feel how good it feels. Listen to yourself being pleased with yourself.

5 Really imagine as fully as you can what it will feel like when you are happy and proud of yourself. Ask yourself what you have learned. Where has the anxiety gone? How do you feel about that past event now you have successfully completed it?

6 Now take that knowledge and understanding back to the spot you marked as your present. Face the future event. How do you think about the event now? Now you have the value of hindsight before the event, does it change how you approach the event?

Usually the answer is most definitely yes, it makes it much easier!

Create your ideal life

If you found that exercise valuable for one incident, how valuable would it be if you could look at your life in the future in the same way? Interested? You would be missing a great opportunity if you weren't.

To get the best from the following exercises, relax and enjoy and really experience your future as fully as you can; see, feel, hear, taste and smell what it is like. Savour, luxuriate, and breathe in the experience until it is part of every muscle and cell. Thoughts of a great future are very empowering!

What would your life be like if you lived out of your values? If you designed it so that your values were completely present and fulfilled? What would your perfect day, your perfect life be like, ten years from now?

Your ideal day – ten years from today

Imagine your timeline in front of you. Notice where the present is and where the future is. Pick out a point ten years into your future. (If you are uncomfortable with the thought of planning ten years into the future, choose a shorter timeframe that seems right to you.) Then stand in the present on your timeline. As you stand in the present, say your five most important values to yourself, feel how wonderful it is when those values are present. Breathe in those values until they are a part of every cell, every muscle, every part of you. Feel them filling you up with pleasure and happiness.

When you have a strong sense of being fully present and in tune with your values go along your timeline until you are ten years in the future.

Imagine you are living fully your ideal day, fulfilling all your values. Feeling healthy and resourceful. See what you would see, feel what you would feel, hear what you would hear. If there are smells, smell them and if there are tastes, taste them. Describe your life as fully as you can. These questions may help you.

- How is it?
- Where are you?
- What is the weather like?
- What is your home like?
- What kinds of people are in your life?
- What are you doing?
- How are you making money?
- How are you in relation to yourself?
- How are you in relation to others?
- What contributions are you making to life?
- How does life feel?
- What do you appreciate about your life?

Write this out in full in your notebook. Include at the top of the page the date it will be in ten years from now. Keep it for future and frequent reference. After all, a perfect day is something to be savoured and enjoyed.

Your ideal day – five years from today

Start at the present and breathe in your values again. Once you know they are fully with you go forward on your timeline to that wonderful day ten years in the future. Fully experience the pleasure of it again and slowly move back five years.

How will it be in five years when you are on course for your ten year goals? What steps will you still have to take to get there? What changes will you still have to make? Ask the same type of questions as before to fully experience yourself and your life in five years' time.

Write this out in full in your notebook. Include at the top of the page the date it will be in five years from now. Keep it for frequent reference.

Ideal days on the way – stop at three years from today and one year

Repeat the exercise, this time going forward to ten years, coming back to five years then three years. Stop and explore your ideal day. Put yourself in it as completely and fully as you can. See what you would see, hear what you would hear and feel what you would feel. If there are smells, smell them, if there are tastes, taste them.

What is that ideal day like in three years' time? Are you on track for your five and ten year goals? Take note of what you need to do to make your long term vision happen. Look back at the 'you' in the present. What are the changes that the younger you could make to get to where you are at the three year, five year and ten year future?

Come back down your timeline until you are one year into the future. Stop and look forward to three, five and ten years and look back at the present. Get as full an idea as you can of what you need to do to achieve your ideal future.

What advice and direction would the 'you' of the future give to the younger you? What knowledge, support and advice would you give to the present self? You have the opportunity of hindsight; use it to tell yourself the things you know would help you.

Help yourself by identifying what you need to do in the present to get what you want in the future. Again write it out in detail. You will find this information useful now and in the future.

> You have a great future. To create it you will need to start making changes now.

Are your values compatible with who you are?

What else could block you? Just as conflict between your values can cause you stress and problems, so can conflict between your values and your idea of who you are.

Try it now

Ask yourself:

- Who am I?
- Are there parts of me I can change?
- Are there parts of me I would change?

- Does my ideal life fit in with who I am as a person?
- Does who I am match who I would need to be to live that life?
- What do I want to say, see or feel about myself to live that life?
- Are there any changes I want to make to my values?
- Are there any changes I want to make to myself?

If you want to reassess your values, go back and do it now. If you want to make any changes to yourself, keep reading.

Your life purpose

As well as knowing who you are and what your values are, do you have a sense of a mission in life? Does the future you have created that fulfils your values give you an idea of your life's purpose? Do you know what your purpose is? What is your personal mission statement or vision for your life? You may want to explore this by asking yourself, ' *What would I like to see written in my obituary?*' The purpose of this is not to think about death but more to think about what your life meant.

Try finishing this sentence with the first five things that come into mind.
Here is someone who lived their life...

For many people their life purpose is connected to their spirituality – spirituality that does not necessarily involve religion but may be more to do with a sense of connection to something bigger than themselves, something other than the tangible here and now, something beyond the present experience. You may have a symbolic representation for it. It could be the flame of a candle, a bright light, the earth. It may be a sense of a higher self whose guidance you value. Like values, there is no right or wrong spirituality. Just what is right for you.

Keeping powerful

If you have found your ten year future has energised and motivated you, it is very valuable to keep that vision of your future fresh in your mind as often as you can. As well as writing it out with as much detail as you can and referring back to it, you may want to give yourself a symbol to keep in your mind.

You could give yourself a symbol for the 'you' of the present and a symbol for the 'you' of the future. A symbol for who you are now and a symbol for you in your ideal life helps you compare how far you have come and how far you have to go. Knowing who you are now and who you want to be, keeps you on course. The symbol helps bring you back to your course if you have lost your way or have any doubts. If you have any questions or doubts about decisions or actions, find out if it is compatible with your symbol. If it's not, you may be causing yourself internal conflict and stress.

Here are some examples. You can probably add to them and come up with one of your own:

- animals
- cars
- trees
- musical instruments
- books
- poems
- months of the year
- seasons
- water
- landscapes.

Discover the power of symbols

Choose the type of symbol that appeals to you. If you choose musical instruments for example, close your eyes and let a musical instrument that represents who you are now come into your awareness. Make it as real and detailed as possible.

- What kind of instrument is it?
- How does it sound?
- What is it made of?

- How does it feel in your hands?
- What is its history?
- What is special about it?
- What kind of notes, music does it play?

Your symbol may come from any of your senses; when it becomes known, investigate it. Fully get to know that symbol of who you are at present. Ask yourself:

- Does it have an image or a sound?
- What colours are there?
- Are they deep, pastel, bright – how would you describe them?
- Does it have a name or a tone associated with it?
- What kind of smell does it have?
- How does it feel, are you aware of any textures, temperatures, energies?

Now get in touch with your future symbol. Ask yourself the same questions and consider, how good do you feel when you see that future symbol? The more you know about your symbol, the more powerful it will be for you. Your future symbol should act as a beacon of light or a siren calling you forward. It should inspire you, filling you with hope, confidence and determination.

Case study

When we asked our seminar group to draw an animal as a symbol of themselves as they understood themselves to be at present, Maria drew herself as a mouse. She explained her drawing was of a small, warm bodied, grey mouse with soft fur and a long tail. Her mouse smelt of old potatoes. When she did make a sound it was a small squeak. Her mouse was often there in the room quietly in the corner watching what went on but it went unnoticed. The mouse was intelligent and quick but did not like to make herself the centre of attention. She wanted to stay hidden. Often she was timid and unsure of herself. But she scurried about finding food to keep her family fed and well cared for. The mouse wanted to go outside the house but couldn't leave her family. She was also scared of what might be out there.

▶

In contrast, Maria's future symbol was a wise old owl. Sharp eyed, who watched the world with tolerance and objectivity. Occasionally the owl would ruffle its brown and speckled feathers and others would look up in admiration. The owl could be a predator if it chose to be, but it rarely would. It is much happier just watching and knowing. When the other people and animals heard its 'twit twoo' it would bring them comfort. They would know the old knowledge was safe and nearby. Others would come to her for advice. Generations of owls would remember her with respect and speak about the great contributions she made.

For Maria, the owl became a symbol of what she wanted for herself. The owl allowed her to be reminded of what was possible for her. The owl gave her focus; when she compared where she was with where she wanted to be the owl gave her feedback, and it allowed her a kind of fellowship. She knew other people were on their own parallel paths like herself. Every time she saw or heard an owl she was reminded of what her values and vision were. The ceramic owl that she put in her bedroom, and the owl fridge magnet were permanent and powerful motivators for her to achieve what she knew would make her truly happy.

Keep in touch with your vision

Like Maria, find mementoes that bring your future symbol to mind. Write your values in the front of your diary and draw something that represents your symbol. Refer to it every week at least. If you prefer you could compile a tape with all your favourite pieces of music that incorporate your vision of where you want to be and who you want to be. Let it inspire you. Let the music be in tune with that vision so that your vision remains alive and fresh in your mind. You have experienced how powerful being in touch with your values and your vision for the future can be. Use it, tap in to it every day.

You have so much potential: make sure you direct it in the right direction.

Another way to keep yourself motivated and connected to what you want is to make a large colourful collage of everything you want in your future.

Wake up to your ideal future every day

Create a collage for your bedroom wall. Every day when you wake up and see that collage you will be reminded of what you want and where you are going.

Get together a pile of old magazines and go through them cutting out pictures of what you want in your future. Once you have found a picture of something that represents one of the qualities you want, stick them to a board. When the board is full, put it up where you can see it.

Summary

If we live our lives with conflicting values the result may be unhappiness, lack of energy, maybe even depression. Living life in total harmony with our values will bring about contentment and joy. We can start to use our values as a guide to taking the 'here and now' steps necessary to reach our future goals. We may be able to visualise our life's mission and purpose and work towards fulfilling it in a way that inspires and motivates us.

- Often people live according to others' values, not their own.
- Once you have identified your values you can use them to create a life that is right for you.
- Visualise living your perfect life according to your values and it will enhance your growth and encourage change.
- Conflict between your values and your sense of self can block your journey forward.
- An awareness of your life's purpose will help the process of change.

A vision of your ideal future fresh in your mind can keep you powerful.

5 Recognise how you Create your Life

'The real voyage of discovery consists not in seeking new lands but in seeing with new eyes.'

Marcel Proust

Now you know what you want, let's address the ways to make it happen. When you understand where you are today and the process by which you got there, you can begin to use the same processes to get you where you want to go. The biggest barrier and greatest challenge to creating a fantastic life for yourself, is yourself. Most of us do our best with the choices we give ourselves but often the choices we give ourselves are very limited by the way we view the world.

We view it through personal filters, then respond to our internal experience of the world rather than the world directly. That is why many of the mind magic exercises in the next few chapters require you to go inside yourself, because that is where the answers lie. The causes and the answers to your life are not out there in events, possessions or in other people; they are inside you. Regardless of circumstances, you are the one who creates your experience. Your life is a product of your thinking. When you start to accept and understand that, you can begin to direct your internal experience to achieve that wonderful life you want.

Regardless of circumstances

This chapter will start the process of helping you understand that you create your own version of reality for yourself. When you understand how this happens you can re-programme your inner experience to be a very supportive one. You now know the power of your mind from the previous exercises. You know how empowering it can be when you feel good and are focused on what you want and know is right for you. Your mind can hamper or exquisitely nurture you depending on how you direct it. Learn to direct it usefully.

Consider this list of names; Kurt Cobain, John Belushi, Ernest Hemingway, Marilyn Monroe, Michael Hutchence, Janis Joplin. What they have in common is great success in their field. They had money, fame, glamour, choice of partner, talent and recognition. These may not meet your value criteria, or even theirs, but you could imagine in their circumstances they would experience some sense of happiness and satisfaction.

Contrast their fate with that of someone like Simon Weston or Christopher Reeve. Simon, the subject of a series of BBC documentaries, was one of the Welsh Guards who was very badly burnt when the *Sir Galahad*, the ship he was being transported on, was tragically bombed in Bluff Cove in the Falkland Isles. Simon managed to escape the blaze but was left disabled and disfigured, after forty six per cent of his body was burned. Similarly, the late Christopher Reeve, best remembered as the actor who played Superman, was an action man who enjoyed and valued his independence and control of his life. Everything he thought was important to him disappeared one day when he became paralysed from the neck down, after being thrown from his horse.

Two different sets of people, one set who seemed to have it all; the other two, tragic victims of circumstances. Yet those who seemingly had everything were the true victims of their own inner experience, an experience of dissatisfaction and unhappiness. In the end their abundant circumstances were empty and meaningless for them. Most of them suffered from self-destructive behaviour and early death, some by suicide, others wasted in drug- or alcohol-related obliteration. Although every one of them seemed to have everything going for them, their inner experience defeated them.

Again contrast their inner experience with that of Simon Weston. Instead of curling up in a corner and feeling sorry for himself, Simon put his personal tragedy to good use and now lives his life to the full. In Simon's eyes his terrible misfortune became the *'best thing that ever happened to me, all these opportunities and positive things came out of it'*. By drawing on his inner resources and his positive mental attitude, Simon turned his accident and his medical discharge from the army into a catalyst for self-growth. Even though he suffered from depression and heavy drinking in the beginning, he started to take charge of his life. Not content with being thought of as a victim, he faced his fears and found the potential within himself. He wanted to be happy in life, something he has achieved. He enjoys a rich and fulfilling family life with a wife and three children, and devotes his life to fundraising for disadvantaged groups. So far he has raised over £20 million. For Simon and those who come into contact with him, life has become richer because of the accident. All of this is down to Simon's mental attitude and his approach to his circumstances.

Similarly, Christopher and his family decided his life was more important to them than being a victim to tragic circumstances. Knowing the prognosis, Christopher was involved in making the decision not to turn off his own life support system. After that he learned to cope with the loss of his old life and the possibilities of a new one. During the remaining years of his life he maintained a positive attitude that one day he would walk again and used his status as a powerful voice for the paraplegic disabled. Although he had a great deal of support from friends and family, in the end it came down to how Christopher managed his emotional state. His attitude and ability to adapt and face his new circumstances came down to his mental ability to help and motivate himself. Christopher was the victim of a tragic accident but he chose not to be a victim in life.

> It is not the circumstances that make a difference; it is the meaning that we give to them.

We face the same challenges

Although both Simon and Christopher's mental strength and flexibility were tested to the limit in extreme circumstances, we face the same challenges of motivating and helping or hindering ourselves every day. Like Viktor Frankl, Stephen Hawking and many other people whom we never get to hear about, the ability to choose to go beyond surviving and living to the full is a personal decision. Each of these people focused on what was possible for them and then found ways to achieve it. They had belief in themselves and an interpretation of the circumstances around them that motivated rather than floored them. They had every reason to be victims in life, to give up and rage against the world. Instead they lived their lives as purposefully as they could. They are living proof to the truth of the expression: *'There is nothing either good or bad, but thinking makes it so'* (Shakespeare).

How we think it 'is'

It is comforting to believe we can only react to what is happening to us, but unfortunately the price of that comfort is that we become a victim of our circumstances and a victim in our life. It is not our circumstances that knock us down or have us jumping for joy, it is the meaning that we give to them. Our response to things is far more important than what is actually happening. If we judge it a good thing then that is what it becomes; if we judge it a bad thing then that is what it is in our mind.

Imagine waking up one night and seeing a stranger in your bedroom; imagine the fear that would arise. It probably would be quite terrifying and intense. What would happen if you eventually realised the stranger was only the overcoat back from the drycleaners that you hung up on the wardrobe door. Relief would flood through you and eventually the fear would subside. That fearful state arose because of what you were telling yourself and seeing in your mind's eye. When you told yourself, 'it's ok, it's only a coat', the fear subsided. When you told yourself, 'I am in danger' and pictured yourself being harmed, the potential of what you imagined could happen brought on the panic.

It is not the event that makes the difference but rather our response to it. There is no doubt waking up to a stranger in your room in the middle of the night would not be high on many people's wish list but your ability to handle the situation would be greatly enhanced if you were calm and composed and not paralysed with fear. When you have the ability to choose your response it makes a difference to how you handle the situation and helps you cope with difficulties.

If Simon and Christopher had given their circumstances the meaning that their life was over, that is what would have floored them – not their accident. It is not the event that makes the difference but rather what we make it mean. We are all living in our own personal myth of how life *'is'*. We think we are living in a true objective reality, but *each* one of us has a different true and objective reality. All that anxiety, worry and fear exists in our thinking. In the pictures and stories we tell ourselves in our head, in the knot in our stomach. We generate it for ourselves, yet we honestly believe it is real. Teresa's imagined outcome of Jim leaving her was 100% real in her mind, an unavoidable truth that would come about from her talking to him about his time on the computer.

Ultimately, there is no such thing as reality, just our inner experience of it. We are the ones who create our own experience by the meaning we give to things. If we think it is so, then for us it is. All those barriers of worry, fear, anxiety and guilt exist in our internal experience. It's in our head, not out there, yet we convince ourselves it is real.

Creating our imaginary world

The way we experience the world is through our senses. Through what we hear, see, feel, taste and smell. These are our sources for receiving information about the world. As we experience what is happening around and inside us through our senses we give it meaning.

Many of the meanings and responses we assign will come from our own experiences and past. Each of us is unique. One person may believe dogs are great fun to be around and no family is complete without one. They could never trust a partner who did not like dogs. Another might believe people who talk to their dogs or treat them like children are in serious need of help. Another person may consider that dogs are dangerous and do not belong in a house. If each person were asked to think about a dog, each of them might have their own idea of what a dog looks like, what it sounds like, what it smells like. The feelings they experience will also be unique to each of them.

Our meanings guide behaviour

Their memories of past experiences with *dog* will be very much present in their belief and their response to *dog* today. How they respond to *dog* internally will affect how they respond to *dog* externally. If, in their mind, their internal experience of dog is a large, growling, aggressive monster, the memory of a bad past experience, they are hardly likely to respond with enthusiasm if a pooch runs up to greet them. Alternatively, if their internal notion of a *dog* is the cute pup that was an important and loving member of their family, then they will probably be enthusiastic and happy to 'oh' and 'ah' over someone else's best friend. They are responding to their own past experience of dog and not the external one.

Are you sure what you thought you saw?

Please read the following sentence:

FINISHED FILES ARE THE RESULT OF YEARS OF SCIEN-TIFIC STUDY COMBINED WITH THE EXPERIENCE OF MANY YEARS.

Now count the Fs in the sentence. Count them one time only. Do not go back and count them again.

Question

How many Fs are there?

Answer

There are six Fs. However, because the F in OF sounds like a V, it seems to disappear. Most people perceive only three Fs in the sentence. Our conditioned habitual patterns restrict us from being alert as we should be. Frequently, we fail to perceive things as they really are.

The process for creating a predictable world

The beliefs that we have, the 'rules' that we follow all act as guidelines for making meaning and regulating our behaviour. Once we have a guideline in place we organise our attention to make sure we find evidence that supports our meaning. In other words we like to be right. That means we can bet on our world being a predictable and controllable place. Not necessarily a happy place, unless we have very supportive guidelines in place, but certainly a less uncertain experience.

Figure 5   An example of closure

The mind likes to know where to file things

Driven by the need for certainty and predictability, the human mind looks for patterns, meanings and interpretations. Unidentified things are chaotic to our sense of order and predictability. What did you see when you looked at Figure 5? It's an example of closure – your mind likes to make sense of things. If you identify the series of black and white blobs as a picture of a dog you can mentally file it away as something you recognise. You no longer have to think about it, you know what it is and you know what it's all about based on past experience.

Your unconscious organises your world

Many of these processes happen unconsciously. There is so much information around for us to pay attention to, to sort out what is important, what is irrelevant, what is dangerous, what is worth investigating. In some circumstances our very survival depends on making split-second decisions. Should we stay and fight or take to our heels as quickly as possible? These are useful processes for helping us regulate our world. If you had to consciously pay attention to everything, from the weight of your body in the chair, the rate of your breathing, regulating the beat of your heart or pumping of your blood, never mind what else is going on in the environment outside you, you would go nuts. Information overload at its best.

Try it now

Relax and get comfortable. Turn your attention from your reading to your breathing. Quiet yourself and go inside.

- Tune in to the sound of your breathing. Notice how you are breathing... Are you breathing in through your mouth or your nose? Pay attention to how often you breathe. Follow the route of the breath – how far do your lungs expand? Does your breath reach your abdomen? Is the inhale as deep as the exhale or as long? Are you exhaling through your mouth or your nose? What temperature is your breath as it enters your body, as it moves down into your lungs, as you exhale? What else can you notice about your breathing?
- What else is going on inside you? How are you feeling? Slowly turn your attention to each part of your body in turn. Starting with your scalp, just notice how it feels. What is its temperature? Is there any tension there? Move down your body, do the same for your forehead, your eyes. Notice the relaxation of the muscles at the side of your eyes, then turn your attention to your nose, your mouth, your jaw. Move through your body until you get to your toes.
- Turn your attention to how you are sitting. Feel the pressure of the surface beneath you, the temperature of your skin, the weight and feel of your clothes on your body.
- What about the sounds you can hear if you tune in? Are there sounds coming from inside the room, perhaps a clock ticking or outside, the wind against a window, bird song or music or voices?
- How much of this were you aware of before you turned your attention to it?

Our limited attention

Imagine trying to pay attention to all of that at once. Impossible! We can only pay attention to what we think is important and ignore what is not. We have unconscious guidelines for what is worth devoting our precious attention to. Mothers can often ignore the racket of their children fighting and squabbling, unless it gets serious. In fact, we are quite limited to what we can pay attention to consciously. Which is why we are so selective. Back in the 1960s a researcher called Miller suggested we could only cope with an average of seven things at once, and we all know people who seem to be limited to one item at a time, especially if it involves a television!

Organising our world

We sort information by getting rid of some of it – although not everything is lost. Some information goes directly into the subconscious without us being aware of it unless there is a good reason to pay conscious attention to it. At a party you may hear your name being mentioned in another conversation: all of a sudden you are tuned into what is being said about you. Otherwise the information gets stored away just in case we need it later. This is why hypnotism can be so effective for helping witnesses recall valuable information stored in their unconscious mind. It gets into the cupboards of our mind and finds out what is gathering cobwebs there.

The cupboard of the unconscious

Although we may not be aware of what is in the cupboard of the unconscious, it does not mean it is irrelevant. Often the programmes that shape our thinking are running there at an unconscious level. So even if we are not aware of what filters and guidelines we are using to make meaning and regulate our behaviour, they still influence us. The ones we know about we can at least refute or find evidence to question. The ones we don't know about can have the greatest power since they are never contested.

> The mind is not a cluttered broom cupboard; it is a highly efficient and organised system. It's just that sometimes the way it is organised may not be the most useful way.

Selective perception

Our attention is like a searchlight that only illuminates what we have told it to. We programme our senses and our brain to find evidence to validate our thinking.

If we believe we are a failure we will set ourselves unrealistically high standards, then notice all the times we fail to exceed those standards. If we believe we are not good enough we put our successes down to luck and our failures down to us. If we believe in ourselves we will give ourselves realistic goals and credit for attempting and learning something new. We notice our successes and celebrate our attempts. All of it is there but we programme our attention to notice only what validates our biases.

> 'Two men look out their prison window; one sees mud, the other sees stars.'
>
> Anonymous

The advantage of positive programming

Too often we are looking or listening out for what we want to avoid rather than what we want in our life. What we want to avoid is actually what we can create for ourselves – because that is what we are looking and listening out for. Our searchlight finds it out. The mind does not recognise negatives. If you're told 'don't think of that itch on your back', the first thing you do is turn your attention to your back and check out if there is an itch, and then with that picture in your mind, tell yourself not to think of it. Don't think of the last time you had sex, and what comes to mind? When you tell yourself not to do something, or to avoid something, that is what you bring to your attention. Instead of avoiding it, it's in your face. That means a lot of your precious attention is taken up with what you don't want rather than what you do want in your life.

What we don't want to know

We are also very talented at reshaping or distorting information so that it fits into the categories and guidelines we've already decided on. It's quicker and easier that way to deal with new information and it means you don't have to think too hard or break outside your comfort zone.

Ponder the fate of a young and very adventurous sixteenth century Spaniard who returned home from travels in South America proudly wearing a rubber cape. Unfortunately, he was tried and sentenced to death for witchcraft, all because the rain could not pass through his new 'mac'. The best way his judge and jury could make sense of this new information, his magical mac, was to distort it to accommodate the beliefs they already had. Since they had no knowledge of rubber but knew all about witches and black magic, he must have been a witch. It made perfect sense to them!

The people of Hartlepool are still called 'monkey hangers' today because of their sense-making in the past. During the Napoleonic Wars a poor bedraggled monkey was shipwrecked on their coast. The townspeople consequently hanged the monkey. Since they had never seen a Frenchman before they presumed the monkey was a French spy and as such should dangle on the end of a rope.

Like the people of Hartlepool, what you think is a perfectly sane and rational interpretation may be very much off base. You distort it to fit in with what you already think you know to be true. Often there is more than one way to see something.

Figure 6   There is more than one interpretation – what is it, a B or 13?

Look at Figure 6. Did you notice that you saw what you expected to see? What you expect to see may not be the only possibility.

We hear a sound we identify as a door closing, but louder than usual. We make it mean that someone is angry with us: they are annoyed, they might fire us, they might leave us. We begin a conversation in our head. We start to feel upset, apprehensive and angry and wonder, *'What have I done?'* or think *'They are unreasonable'* or *'They might get us into trouble'* or *'I'll get them first'* or ... The possibilities from a door closing louder than usual are endless. We respond to what we made the sound mean. Then get upset at them for what they did to us!

We don't get a job we applied for and we make it mean all sorts of things. We can blame ourselves: we are not good enough, no one will ever want us, we are female/male, under/over qualified, too young/old, too tall/short, fat/thin and so on. We can go the other way: the interviewer was prejudiced and an idiot. She was frightened we would steal her job. He was intimidated by someone older/younger, more qualified or experienced. Recognise it?

You may want to start questioning some of the assumptions and meanings you have assigned to events. Could there be other explanations: explanations that help you rather than defeat you? Remember you are not looking for the *'truth'*, just another possibility that helps you move forward.

Generalising to support our beliefs

The third way we make our world a predictable place is to take a little bit of information and make it mean a whole lot more. We make all sorts of assumptions from a small piece of information. Generalisations are made from a few observations or statements and extrapolated. Going back to the example of *dog*, if you believe dogs are great because of a happy experience when you were younger you will tend to generalise that all dogs are friendly and good fun. In your mind an aggressive one is an exception; there must be a good reason for its bad behaviour. However, if you believe dogs are dangerous and not to be trusted because of a previous incident you will be waiting for the friendly animal to turn, believing that if you give it long enough eventually it will.

We also make the same type of generalisations about people (substitute *men* or *women* or *Welsh* or *French* people etc. for *dog*). This is how stereotypes come into being. We paint a full picture of who and what they are from a couple of small details. If we have a stereotype of a certain type or group of people, how often do we make it a self-fulfilling prophecy by our own approach to them? Then, of course, we reinforce our opinion.

Beliefs about others

In 1968 two American researchers Rosenthal and Jacobson ran an experiment on the power of self-fulfilling prophecies. They told elementary school teachers that some of the children in their class could be expected to improve their performance significantly during the school year, on the basis of their scores in a test. In fact this was completely untrue. The children's names were randomly selected and were no more likely to be more intelligent or likely to improve than any other child in the class.

At the end of a school year, the children's IQs were assessed in a real test. Those randomly selected children who were expected to do well by their teachers showed a marked real gain of over 10 IQ points more than did other children. A self-fulfilling prophecy. The teachers' beliefs about the 'special' children came true. Apparently, the good impressions and expectations of improvement by the teachers were translated into real improvement, probably because the teachers paid particular attention to those children whom they expected to perform well.

We create other people's behaviour

How often do we create self-fulfilling prophecies because of our own behaviour? If we believe someone is unfriendly or aggressive they may well behave that way. However, they may be reacting just as we expect, not because they are really unfriendly or aggressive but because we behaved in an unfriendly and defensive way towards them. Similarly, our expectations of positive behaviour may often be confirmed by subsequent experience simply because our own behaviour was more positive to begin with. If we trust someone they are likely to return that trust. If we like someone then they are likely to like us. If we are dismissive of someone then they are likely to be dismissive back. What about those generalisations, the stereotypes we believe about other people? How often do we make them happen because of our own behaviour? We play our part in the system. Our beliefs, expectations and behaviours are returned to us.

Mind reading

How often do you assume you have great psychic powers? The answer is probably quite often. It can start as early as childhood. We imagine we know what is going on in someone else's mind: *'Dad must be angry with me. He looks bad tempered and annoyed. I must have upset him by being bad.'* What is really going on is Dad is concerned about a project he is working on, and is lost in thought about it, but we have decided it has to be our fault. We believe we think we know what others are thinking: *'She doesn't like me'*, *'He said that just to hurt me'*, *'They think I'm stupid.'*

What are the possibilities you could be wrong? You could actually check out what someone was thinking, what they meant when they said this or that. You may be surprised and delighted by what is going on in their world. The odds are what you are imagining could be very different from what is going on for them.

Our version is not the only version

We firmly believe that we know what we have represented in our head and body is an absolutely unbiased, objective record, and that everyone else has or should have the same representations in their heads and bodies. Which is why you can hear someone else tell a story of something that happened when you were both present, yet you find their version of events totally unrecognisable. So, when you are convinced your partner, friend, colleague or relation appears to be a consummate liar, stop and consider that they are living in a world of their own, just as you are. They and you are in a world of your own inner experience. We forget that what we know is only a filtered version of what has been and is happening.

Our filters shape our world

Our filters of personal beliefs, attitudes, values and motivations shape how we approach and live our lives. Humans are amazingly talented at justifying their nice, ordered world. It is one of the basic drives to have a safe, predictable, certain environment, which our theories and beliefs allow. But, and it is a very big but, it also closes our eyes and ears, nose and taste buds to a fantastic variety of new experiences and possibilities. It keeps our world neat and tidy and manageable and totally subjective.

> When we change our filters, we change our world.

Differentiating our conditioning

Many of the beliefs we have are not grounded in reality but instead come from our conditioning. The messages we send ourselves are like tapes playing in the back of our mind. They may not originally have been our own messages. They may have come from elsewhere: parents, the media, friends, school. These messages from outside are part of our conditioning. Some of these conditioning messages may have worked well for us, others not. Once we have identified what belongs to us and what belongs to others, we can choose what we want to believe. We can begin to play new tapes that support, nurture and empower us.

Fitting in

Many of these beliefs and rules of behaviour have come from our parents. When we are little we have no way of looking after ourselves. We learn that we have to depend on others for our survival. Although we have to learn to let others know what we need, part of that learning is behaving in ways that please them and get them to accept and take care of us. Fitting in is one of the most powerful survival tools we learn when growing up. It's only natural when we are young and defenceless, to adopt the behaviours, attitudes and beliefs that our carers hold dear. Our survival depends on it.

Fitting in and learning the rules is a major task for anyone. The rules of one family, one culture may not apply elsewhere. As well as shaking hands when they meet, Tibetans bump foreheads. The Inuit, as most people know, rub noses. Masai tribesmen spit at each other when they meet and when they part. Newborn babies are spat on as a sign of good luck, and traders spit at customers when a bargain is sealed! Try operating to those rules and see how popular and welcome you are outside of the Masai tribe.

Each family, each culture has its own set of rules. As a child you adopt them to fit in. As an adult you can make choices about your beliefs and the 'rules' you want to follow. What may have been useful for you as a child may have passed its 'sell by' date for you as an adult. You may not be aware of what tapes are running in the background. When you begin to bring them under that searchlight you can examine them and decide which ones are useful. You may have adopted the ideas behind them without choosing to as an adult, or the rebel in you may have rejected them completely just because your parent adopted them. Listen to what is useful and think about what you would like to pass on to future children. When you start to decide for yourself what you consciously want in your life, you are making choices for others around you, perhaps even generations to come. You can choose to empower yourself, and in turn other people, or you can continue to pass on what was passed on to you.

Family sayings

Listen for the family sayings that may have wormed their way into your unconscious. These can reflect the ways to 'fit in' in your family. Many will have been forgotten, but they may be there whispering in the background, especially when you are about to break one. These family sayings and the ideas they reflect can be the reason behind the 'rules of behaviour' and the meanings you assign to events in your life. They can be very powerful and very much taken for granted as the 'right' way to be unless you examine them and ask, *'is this useful to me now?'*

Occasionally in our workshops we come across great ones like, *'You can be anything you want to be', 'Have faith in yourself and you'll get there',* but these are exceptions. On the whole the majority of family sayings are not very helpful for building self-confidence or pride in being successful. Many of the sayings imply it is *'wrong'* or *'bad'* to improve your situation and get what you want or get better at something. Even more inhibiting, many of the sayings suggest it is *'naughty'* or *'bad'* to even want anything more or question what you have. Somehow there is something amiss to dream and to want something different. Very few families tell their children they are perfect as they are, that they deserve to have all their dreams fulfilled.

Often the 'elders and betters' have very positive intentions when criticising or reprimanding a child. They want the child to learn new behaviours, to respect other people, to fit in and be happy. Unfortunately the child does not realise this and takes the criticism of the behaviour as condemnation of themselves.

In some eastern cultures there is a strong superstition that the evil eye may fall on any child who is beautiful or special. Parents are guarded in their praise in case pride in the child attracts the attention of the evil eye. Charms are sold to protect the wearer from harm. Parents are careful with compliments, just in case retribution comes the child's way. Perhaps we have a similar superstition we have forgotten about. The behaviour remains but the initial curse of the evil eye is forgotten. For most people it seems easier to criticise and comment on what could be improved rather than what is just wonderful and worthy of praise. Perhaps they see it as safer for the child. Since you are the only you, you can only be the perfect you. There is no one to compare you with. If you ever want to compare yourself with anyone, the only person who has the same attributes, circumstances etc., is you. If you have to compare yourself, compare yourself with how far you have come.

Try it now

Remember your family sayings. Here are a few we have come across – sound them out and add your own.

- You get nothing for nothing!
- No pain, no gain!
- Better the devil you know!
- Nice children don't ask!
- I want doesn't get!
- People are starving; you should be grateful!
- You don't know how lucky you are!
- Who do you think you are?
- Ideas above his station!
- Some sort of smart alec?
- The grass is always greener on the other side!
- Too big for your boots!
- Beggars can't be choosers!
- Some people are never satisfied!
- Nice girls don't discuss money!

Over the next few days you will probably find more and more sayings come to mind. As they do, consider their meanings for you.

If one of your family sayings was *nice girls don't discuss money*, what did this mean to you? What else did you take this to mean about being nice, about being a girl, about money? How significant is money to you? Do you suffer conflict or guilt about money – one part wanting it, the other criticising you for wanting it? What would happen if you were to discuss money – then and now? Negative commands actually put the idea in children's heads making it even harder for them to comply.

If you were told as a child *big boys don't cry*, what other things did you think big boys did or didn't do? What would happen if you did cry – then and now? Do you have a conflict about expressing your sad and hurt feelings?

If you have some empowering family sayings, pass them on to other people. You may even consider making up some new ones for your own family.

- You only fail if you never attempt it.
- You can't win unless you enter the race.
- Mistakes are learning opportunities.

Think about other things that were said to you as you grew up

- Be careful.
- Don't be selfish.
- Don't answer back.
- Hurry up, you're holding us up.
- You're stupid, clumsy, irresponsible, bad, wicked, naughty, dirty, an idiot.

Or how about some helpful ones

- You'll do ok.
- You can do it. If you get stuck, I'll help.
- You're always perfect to me.
- You're wonderful, special, funny, clever, fantastic, great.

Learning what to believe

When you think about your family sayings or the things that were said to you, what was rewarded, criticised or ignored, what conclusions did you reach about yourself and how you *'should'* behave? What were the beliefs you made about yourself? Most of us tend to feel inadequate, not quite good enough. We lack self-confidence.

However, most of us manage to hide it quite well. We imagine everyone else is fine – it's just us there is a problem with. We can look around and compare ourselves with others and find evidence to support the belief of our inadequacy. Our inner experience of inadequacy and what we deserve stops us from stepping out of our comfort zone. We are so sure of 'failure' we never even try, or give up very quickly when we don't get the results we want straightaway. Yet these unplanned results can be a valuable guide to help us adjust what we need to do to get where we want to go.

Learning to appreciate different outcomes

Part of learning is getting different outcomes for what we set out to achieve. It can let us know it is time to try something different. Some things produce the outcome we planned, other things produce a different outcome than envisaged. It is all a steep learning curve. When we are very young we get praised for trying; then as we get older, mistakes can become *'wrong'* rather than a learning opportunity. No wonder we are so reluctant to try something new if the outcome can lead us to be punished or censured. Usually the parent or teacher is trying to help us to learn. In their own way they are trying to support us – but that is not how we understand it. We give it a different meaning, a meaning about who we are. Any mistake can be taken as evidence supporting that long-held belief that we are stupid, or bad, or naughty, or nasty, or mean. Most of it starts in childhood, but as adults we can make new choices.

'No one can make you inferior without your consent.'
Eleanor Roosevelt

Beliefs about myself

Complete the sentences:

- I am …
- I am not …
- I should…
- I shouldn't…
- It is wrong to…
- I can't …
- I can…
- It is bad for me to …
- It is ok for me to …

When Joan (Chapter 1) uncovered her belief *'It's wrong to be selfish'* she realised she may have misinterpreted her mother's message and intention. Her mother may have been trying to get Joan to share and play with others, to fit in and get on. Her mother may have wanted a little bit of piece and quiet without squabbling. The last thing her mother probably wanted was to give Joan a message that it was wrong to take care of her own needs. It was time for Joan to make a choice as an adult. To take responsibility for the rules she was living her life by.

Changing beliefs

Our beliefs can also be tied up with our idea of who we are. For some people challenging their beliefs means challenging their whole sense of self and the illusions of the world they have created. In defence of their safety and predictability they will do any sort of physical, intellectual, emotional, linguistic high jumps and contortions rather than let go of old, outdated belief structures that hold them in place. Remember the change curve (Figure 4) – shock and denial are the first two stages. The second stage denial seems to be the favourite of most people, for a short time at least. However, the urge to protect and conserve our sometimes fragile sense of self can mean that we hold on to beliefs that hold us back and keep us safely where we have always been. Even though where we have always been can be painful and unproductive for us. It is back to that age-old philosophy: *'Better the devil you know'*. Taking risks and trying new things does not seem part of our cultural philosophy, even though letting go of the old allows so much more room for new things.

Yet our beliefs are not written in stone. There is, nevertheless, a hierarchy of beliefs. Some beliefs *are* very central to our life and who we are. These tend to be linked with our values. These are the beliefs at the core of our essence; perhaps our family, love, the right to freedom. But other beliefs about success and what we deserve are open to change. We may have learned them at an early age, and it may take effort and consistency to unlearn them and replace them with more useful beliefs – but it's possible. Like any habit, you can break it if you choose to. Believing it in the past does not mean you have to believe it in the future!

Clearing out the old to make way for the new

When people are going through changes in themselves and their lives, very often they become motivated to clear out drawers, cupboards, wardrobes, lofts and basements – in order to let air in metaphorically. The mind is not a cluttered broom cupboard, it is a highly efficient and organised system. It's just that sometimes the way it is organised may not be in the most useful way. We can pick up things and never get around to clearing them out again when they are useless or past their best. Making room for the new means clearing out the old first. No one else can clear out your life; you have to do it for yourself.

Questioning the usefulness of what you believe is one of the ways of allowing room for new possibilities to appear. Questions open the cupboard doors to let a fresh breeze in. It is surprising what happens when you open that cupboard door.

Beliefs about men and women

What about the conclusions you reached about men or women? Did you see your mother or father take care of the family and put their own needs last? Did one of your parents continually blame and criticise the opposite sex? What beliefs about men and women do you hold? What are the rules and standards you apply to both? Are they the same for both? Be honest with yourself. The meaning you give to your own and someone else's behaviour may be very dependent on the rules and beliefs you hold.

You may find it is time to reassess your beliefs. The social conditions and gender roles have changed in the last thirty years – perhaps your conditioning may not reflect that. Or you may have unreasonably high or low standards that stop you being happy in relationships. You are the one who makes a picture of how it *should* be, and when the picture of what is happening does not match, you feel upset and let down. You create your own unhappiness and dissatisfaction.

Try it now

Again very quickly run down the list and finish the sentences. Do it quickly and go with what you first say. If you debate with yourself and analyse you may fool or censure yourself. Go for at least three examples for each phrase.

- All men are ...
- Men never ...
- Men always ...
- Men should...
- Men shouldn't...
- All women are ...
- Women never ...
- Women always ...
- Women should...
- Women shouldn't...

Are the standards the same for men and women? Remember, you are uncovering some of the guidelines you have for assigning meaning to things that happen. You are creating a reality with these rules and beliefs. Is it a reality you really want?

Beliefs about other people

What about other people? What are the beliefs and expectations you hold about them? Repeat the last exercise substituting the words 'friends', 'children', 'everyone', for 'men', and 'women'.

Exercise – analysing your beliefs

Look back at your list of beliefs

- How many of them could be founded on misinterpretations?
- How many could have been generalisations? Something that applied only at the time, in that situation or with that person?
- How many are useful to you now?

Go over the list of beliefs again. Pay attention – is it your own voice or someone else's opinion? Ask yourself:

- Who says?
- If it is someone else's opinion, do you agree with it?
- What do you gain by having this belief?
- What do you lose by having this belief?
- If another belief would be more useful?
- How this belief is useful for you?
- If these beliefs are ones that you really want in your life?
- If they will help you achieve what you want out of life?
- If these beliefs will help you build good relationships?
- What do you want instead?

Which beliefs would it be worthwhile cultivating?

1 Make a list of the five key beliefs that have limited you in the past.
2 Make a list of five beliefs that could help you reach your ideal future.

Choosing our own beliefs

We talked earlier in this chapter about the influence of 'fitting in' in childhood and how children misinterpret information, often developing beliefs that do not serve them well for being successful or happy when they are adults. It is comforting to blame it all on our 'elders and betters', but if we want to move forward we are best served by choosing our own beliefs and rules to live by. As adults we have choice and freedom. It may take time and effort to unlearn what we think, but it can be done. It means taking full responsibility for yourself and what you think – *start now!*

What you focus on is what you get

If you are an adult then the odds are you may have had some pretty lousy things happen to you in your life – as well as some very special and wonderful moments. In some seminar situations we hear stories of abuse and sadness that challenge faith in humanity. Some people have had the most destructive childhoods beyond imagining. Are they responsible for what happened to them? No! Is it right that a child is abused? No! But you are no longer a child. If you stay a prisoner of your past, if you stay a victim, if you stay with being wronged you stay in that cycle of helplessness and powerlessness. You condemn yourself to more in the future. You have to live with the consequences of your actions or non-actions, whether it was your fault or not. You are the one who has to live with it. It may not be fair and it may not be right, but unless you change your thinking it will continue to happen. Remember, what you focus on is what you get. If you focus on what happened to you as a victim in the past, that is what you create in your present and future.

Maybe it's time to stop and do something different. The outcome of changing your thinking will be ownership of your life. You may be able to trace a lot of problems or failures in your life back to events that happened when you were a child. But if you want to live your life in freedom and contentment you have to take responsibility for where you are *now*. As Maya Angelou says, '*You did what you knew how to do, and when you knew better, you did better.*' Part of being responsible is taking action to remedy your thinking if it does not inspire you and energise you for achieving a fantastic life for yourself.

There is usually more than one version of reality, so choose one that helps you feel great about yourself. The tools for helping you choose a more useful reality are there in the next chapter. When you feel good to start with, things can only get better.

Summary

When you choose not to be a victim of circumstance or of life, it can empower you and help you move forward. Ultimately, we create our own experience by the responses and meanings we give to things. We filter information by the process of selective perception. We delete, distort and generalise to validate these interpretations and meanings and then forget that we do it. Many of our beliefs and guidelines are no longer useful for us. When we change the filters we can challenge the illusions of the world they have created. The outcome of changing or challenging our beliefs is ownership of our true selves and own lives. We create our own version of reality, so why not create an empowering one?

- The biggest barrier and greatest challenge to self-fulfilment is our own selves.
- It is our response to circumstances that creates happiness and satisfaction – not the circumstances themselves.
- Our past can regulate our present and our future.
- Our beliefs act as filters for making meanings and shaping our world.
- Our filters create our inner experience and guide our behaviour.
- We each have our own truth, so we may as well make ours a supportive one.

There is always more than one way of seeing things.

6 Your Access to the Life you Want

Now you have a strong sense of what stops you moving forward, it's time to start finding ways to handle the obstacles and take action to make that future happen. This chapter will give you the tools to ensure you can and will create your ideal future. In the previous chapter we explored how your life is shaped by your beliefs and the meaning you assign to things. The filters you had in place could help or hinder you. These filters help colour your inner experience of the world. In this chapter you will begin to take charge of *how* and *what* you think. You are about to discover how to change those filters and manage your mind. Many of the following exercises may be very new to you. You may want to enjoy them even more by working through them with a friend.

Discovering states

Consider what it is like to be in a state of excitement. When you are excited and motivated, how do you approach the world? What kinds of results do you usually get when you are excited and motivated? How easy is it to achieve what you want? Compare your state of excitement with your state of frustration. When you are frustrated, what is that same world like? What choices do you have when you are down?

Another way to change your responses is to change your state. When you are in a powerful and inspired state you transcend your beliefs and filters, and this is a great place to start making changes in them.

The power of resourceful states

Some states like excitement, confidence, joy, love, freedom, friendship and power are very resourceful and empowering. They seem to give wings to our abilities and dreams. From here we can create new beliefs, see new possibilities. Other states quagmire us in doubt and lethargy. They keep us stuck, dark and dim in their shadow. When we are depressed, anxious, fearful, guilty, frustrated or stressed we are handicapped; that is when those debilitating beliefs and experiences come to the fore.

Often the same event can happen. The car breaks down, or we lose our wallet, and how we deal with it depends on our state at that time. If we are feeling good and resourceful we just get on with it. We handle it as best we can – it's just a little bump on life's highway. But let the same thing happen when we are in a less resourceful state and it starts to look like the end of the world. We tell ourselves it's part of the grand conspiracy that the world is organising against us personally! We get resentful, feel sorry for ourselves and truly enter victim mode. Those old beliefs get reinforced.

The ebb and flow of our states

Most people just go with the flow of their emotions and states. Yet your state is the combination of how you are thinking and feeling at that moment and how you are experiencing your thinking and feeling. You can change your state by changing your inner experience.

> When you choose to direct how you think and feel you can really support and energise yourself towards achieving your goals.

Changing your internal experience

You can change your internal experience through your sensory systems. We each have our own movie theatre for showing pictures and an amazing sound system for listening. Each body has its own cocktail cabinet of physical feelings that can fizzle and fester accordingly. We even have the added dimensions of smell and taste as part of our senses' repertoire. And we tell the world about it, all the time. You may have noticed when you were doing some of the practical exercises that required you to remember or imagine a time you were asked to see, hear or feel what you were experiencing at the time. *What* and *how* you were seeing, hearing, feeling, smelling and tasting were creating your internal experience, and your inner experience creates your state.

Using our senses

If you listen to what people are saying you will hear what is going on inside them. They will tell you how they are using their senses to think – all unconsciously, because they may not even realise how they are using their sensory systems to create their experience.

Listen out for expressions such as:

- I just tuned out for a moment
- Let's look at the big picture
- That doesn't feel right
- Smell's a bit fishy
- Leaves a nasty taste in your mouth
- An uplifting experience.

These expressions are more than metaphors or chosen by chance. They are descriptions of what is going on inside someone as they let you know *how* they are thinking, how they are constructing their inner experience.

Using imagination and memory to change state

You can change your inner experience by changing *what* you are picturing and telling yourself inside your head. That changes your feelings and your state. You've probably heard how you can cope with the fear of an interview by imagining the interviewer without their clothes on; you may even have used it yourself. That is using your imagination to change your inner experience. Instead of feeling anxious, your internal picture of a naked person behind the desk helped you feel amused – or at least, less intimidated.

Conversely, when we imagine the worst, like Teresa in Chapter 1, our internal pictures and stories of disaster create a state of fear and anxiety. She could, instead, imagine herself being relaxed, confident and in control in any situation. That internal experience would be much more useful for helping her deal with problems and make decisions. She could empower herself by putting her imagination to work, designing a great outcome for herself instead of a scare story.

Try it now

Explore the power of your imagination. Relax and go inside yourself. Imagine you are holding a lemon in your hand. A fresh lemon from the tree. Play with it. Get to know the lemon, discover it. Look at it; notice its colour, the size of it, the texture of its skin, the shape. Feel the weight and shape of the lemon in your hand. Feel the texture, the firmness of the skin, and the temperature of the lemon. Lift the lemon to your nose and smell it. Cut the lemon in half. As the knife slices through the lemon and the juice runs down the side of the knife, smell the tangy aroma of the juice. Pick up a quarter of the lemon and bite into it.

What happens to your mouth? How powerful is your internal experience through using your imagination?

Often we use our imagination for showing the worst outcome instead of the best. Most of us know better, but somehow the negative images and sounds can sometimes seem more powerful and present for us than the positive ones.

The power of memory

Similarly Teresa could have changed her inner experience by replaying a similar past experience where everything turned out well for her. Instead of imagining the worst she could have seen, heard and felt herself going back to a time when she was in a similar type of situation and she accomplished everything she wanted. The good feelings and confidence she may have felt from that time would help her achieve what she wanted in the present situation. Good memories from the past are a great way of creating positive states for yourself.

Ideally we want to make the positive memories and imagination strong and powerful, and the negative ones diminish and fade away. That way our inner experience will help us be at our most resourceful.

Taking charge of our experience

Interestingly, the *way* we see our pictures and *hear* the sounds we hear and *feel* the way we feel can also have a big impact on our internal experience and our state. When we change *how* we see our pictures it can have a ripple effect on what we hear and feel. Similarly when we change *how* we hear something we can change how we see our pictures and experience our feelings. The *how* is what makes one experience powerful and another diminished. If you really want to be able to direct your inner experience, *how* you see your pictures and hear the sound provides the key.

Before you do any of the exercises that follow in this chapter, read them through, then *do* them. The exercises are very powerful when you experience them, not when you read them. Because they are so powerful ensure while you are learning you are *always, always choosing pleasant memories to* work with. It may also be easier to have a friend guide you through them. That way you can just concentrate on doing the exercise and not have to keep referring to the book.

Exercise: discovering how you see, hear and feel

1 Relax ... go inside and remember a time when you were comfortable and relaxed.

2 Think back to where you were and what you were doing. Remember that time when you were relaxed and at ease. And as you begin to remember that experience, and it becomes more and more present for you, becoming clearer and stronger, step back into it and re-live it

again as though it is happening right now. Breath it in, luxuriate in it.
Fully experience those moments of comfort and relaxation.

3 Become aware of *how* you are seeing this memory. Not *what* you are
seeing but *how* you are seeing it. Some people see very clear images,
others feel that they don't really see anything at all, it just seems to
be fleeting impressions. There is no right way of seeing, just your way
– get to know your way.
   • Is it like a movie, is it in motion or is it still like a photograph or a
     slide?
   • Is it in front of you as you watch it or are you in it?
   • Pay attention to the details of *how* it appears.
   • Is it in colour? What about the brightness or the size of it?
   • Is it flat or concave?

4 Turn your attention to any sounds or voices you hear. Again pay atten-
tion to *how* you hear them rather than what you hear.
   • Are the sounds coming from inside your head or outside it?
   • Notice if they are in stereo. Is there more than one voice?
   • What kind of tone and volume do the sounds have?

5 Now become acquainted with the physical feelings you are experienc-
ing.
   • Where do they start?
   • How intense are they?
   • How would you describe them?

It is probably a little strange noticing *how* you see, hear and feel things.
Usually we are so caught up with *what* we are seeing, hearing and feeling
we don't register the *how*. The more you tune in and practise it, the easier
it will become. You may be asking yourself at this point why you need to
do the exercises and wondering if they are purely academic? The answer
is 'no'. *To make it work you need to experience it for yourself.*

> One of the most magical things about the way our brain
> organises information is how we can change what we feel or
> think about things by changing *how* we see and hear and feel
> the memory.

When we change the brightness or size or location of a picture, we are changing the qualities of the image. These qualities of an image are called the visual sub-modalities. Sub-modalities are the small component parts of the pictures, sounds, feeling, smells and tastes we experience. Changing the sub-modalities is just as powerful for changing your state as changing *what* you see, hear and feel.

By changing our sub-modalities we change our experience. We can, if we choose, take the sting out of unpleasant memories by watching ourselves in them, making them smaller and pushing them away from us. We can enhance and magnify good moments and we can even create new memories. All by using these processes. Sub-modality changes, like making the image bigger and brighter, can be a great way of increasing motivation and pleasure. You can make good moments even greater and more empowering just by juicing up the images and sounds.

If you think about many of the films that you have seen, you might find that this is reflected in the ways that movies are made. Happy, fun movies are bright and colourful. Thrillers or suspense movies quite often have a darker hue to them. The atmosphere of the movie is echoed in the way the movie is shot. The soundtrack adds as much to the tone of the movie as the pictures on the screen. These principles are only a reflection of our internal thinking processes.

However, we are all individual and it is worthwhile getting to know how *your* mind and body work, and how they work together. That way you know exactly how to have positive resources whenever you need them.

Using your feelings and body

For many people, the cinema and sound system in their heads, is a new and exciting discovery. They have never consciously been aware of what they have been doing. Other people have neglected the feelings and sensations in their body.

Most humans have a strong self-preservation instinct. If their body or their feelings are telling them *'I feel bad'* they can make the choice not to feel them. They cut themselves off from the neck down so they can be numb to their pain. As a strategy it works, it achieves what is wanted. Unfortunately it has a major downside – when you can't feel pain or distress, neither can you feel joy or pleasure.

Unpleasant feelings are a useful learning experience

If you are feeling bad about something then it is worthwhile paying attention to what is going on. Your feelings are a valuable source of information. Changing state does not necessarily mean ignoring your feelings. It is about learning from them and then going into a more resourceful state for dealing with what you are feeling bad about. When you choose to make changes in your state it can help you deal with what requires attention, rather than ignoring it or getting bogged down by it.

Using the magic of your mind to experiment with visual sub-modalities

Since experimenting inside your thinking may be a new and unusual experience, let's take it slowly and step by step. You may be amazed to discover what you already do and what you can do with your inner experience. We will start with the visual system, that amazing movie theatre in your mind. As you change the quality of your pictures, you will find a difference in your feelings. Here is a list of things you might notice while you pay attention to your feelings.

- How intense is the feeling?
- Does it have a pressure like a 'dead weight', or texture like bubble wrap, or champagne bubbles exploding inside?
- In what location and area do you feel it?
- Do the feelings have size or shape to them?
- Where do they start and end?
- With what emotion would you label this feeling?

Exercise: experimenting with sub-modalities

1 Relax ... get comfortable and turn your attention inward. Go inside yourself. Remember when you were creating your ideal day in ten years. Go back to that time when you were completely happy and excited at the future you had created for yourself. Imagine that experience as if you were there again, as if you were back in time, having that experience over again right now.
   - Notice whether you are running a movie, if it is in motion or still like a photograph or slide.

- Where is it?
- Are you in the picture or are you watching it?
- Is it one image or several?
- Pay attention to all the features of *how* you see what you see.
- What is the size of the picture, the colour, the brightness, the clarity and the energy?
- Does it have a border around it or is it panoramic? Does it look flat or curved?
- Is there anything about it that is particularly noticeable?

2 Now check out the physical feelings in your body.
- Where are they?
- Notice how intense these sensations are.
- What emotion would you call that feeling?

3 Experimentation time – imagine you are bringing the image closer to you. Bring it as close as is comfortable. You may find as it gets closer it gets bigger; if that happens, that's OK.

4 Now notice the physical sensations, the feelings that go along with that closer image.
- Is there a difference?
- Are they more or less intense?
- Are they in the same place, covering the same area?

For most people, a close image and intense feelings go together. The closer the image, the stronger the feelings and the stronger the feelings, the closer the image. If that happens when the image gets closer what happens when you move the images away? For most people, the further away the picture the less intense the feelings. However, experiment with it – everyone is different; there are some people for whom this just does not apply.

There are a lot of other features or sub-modalities that you can change. One that is significant for many people is the brightness of the image. The brightness of an image can boost the impact of their feelings. Dimming it can dampen their feeling.

Be your own movie director

How did you enjoy using mind magic to discover what you can do in your own private movie theatre? You can experiment with the other visual sub-modalities. The more you experiment the more you get to understand how you have set up your own personal system for thinking and feeling. Once you know how everything works in your cinema you can be the director of your own movies. You can change the quality of your experiences and the impact of your memories by changing your sub-modalities.

Remember, sub-modalities are part of your brain organising system. When you change how it is organised you get to a whole new place with the memory. A memory that was once an unpleasant place to visit can be neutralised. You can still have the advantages of what you learned without the unpleasant feelings if you move the image further away from you and make it small and dim. As you experiment you will find changing some sub-modalities intensifies your feelings more than others.

As you continue to experiment with different memories you will probably find the same sub-modality shift affects them all in the same way. If you make an image brighter and it strengthens your feeling, you will probably find that brightening the image does the same for all memories, happy or sad. So you may want to experiment with happy and empowering memories for the moment. Once you are very familiar with your thinking processes, then is the time to re-sort some sour memories.

Try changing your perspective

1 Run your movie of your ideal day into the future on a screen in front of you and experience what it is like to watch yourself as though you were an actor on the screen.

2 This time, step into your movie and watch the action through your own eyes so you are experiencing it again as it happened. This time you are an actor in your film, right in the centre of the action.

For most people watching themselves allows a more detached view compared with being in the movie. Watching yourself is known as a *dissociated* image. This is useful to know and put into practice if you have memories you would like to distance yourself from, memories that you would prefer not to experience strongly again. Magically, very pleasant memories can become even more powerful resources if you step into them, become *associated* and enjoy them in full body, sparkling colour, and surround sound sensation. Keep in mind: if you want to enjoy the memory step into the pleasure; if you want to be less involved step out and watch.

Try changing the size of the picture

Make it as big as you can while still being able to see what is in it. Conversely, make it as small as you can while still being able to make it out. You could also take it down to a dot size. With each change, pay attention to your feelings. What is the relationship between your feelings and the size of the image? When you have finished experimenting with the size put the image back to where you started.

Try changing the colour of the picture

Make the colours alive, vivid and more distinct. Go to the extremes of your paint box. Then try the opposite, watch the colour fade out. Change the picture to a washed out grey. Then change the grey to a more distinct black and white. Again, with each colour transition, pay attention to your feelings. How does the intensity respond? Are the feelings in the same place?

Try changing other sub-modalities

Location of the picture

Still working with the same image of your ideal day, take note of where your image is. Is it in front of you, to the right or the left? Once you have established where the image is check out your feelings again. Now you can move the image to a different place. Keep the image the same closeness, size, brightness, and colour, just move it somewhere else. Now it has moved, what has happened to your feelings? Now you have experimented with the location return your image to where it was originally.

Motion of the picture

See and feel the difference when your picture is a movie compared with when it is still, like a photograph or slide. You could even try speeding up a movie or slowing it down or run it backwards and pay attention to what happens to your feelings.

Other visual sub-modalities to experiment with are the:

- Focus
- Clarity
- Shape
- Number of images.

Experiment with auditory sub-modalities

Although visual images can be powerful at shaping your experiences, our internal sound system can be just as dramatic and useful in its effect. Our auditory system has just as many variables to play with, and in some ways is the one that is most important to 'sound out'. Left to its own devices your auditory system is the one that can be most destructive if you are not aware of what is being played. It can also be incredibly helpful, once you know how it works.

For some reason, most people replay old tapes of nagging and moaning, judgement and condemnation rather than tapes of motivation, support and encouragement. If you are the exception to that generalisation well done: but for many of us our head can be filled with a constant chatter of doom, gloom and apprehension. We may have become so used to this critical voice and name-calling we are hardly aware of how insidious it can be. It can drain us of energy, vitality and hope.

Joan discovered she had a very quiet, soft voice, the voice of herself as a four year old, saying over and over again, *'You can't do it, it's too hard.'* This voice was so subtle, just at the threshold of her conscious awareness, that she had not even realised it was there. It was only when she started to really tune in and pay attention to what she was saying to herself, that she realised this part of her was draining her, destroying her confidence and her ambition. Just by turning up the volume in her little girl's voice she was able to dismiss the voice as a very old tape which belonged to a little four year old and not a competent thirty-five year old woman who had grown and learned many new skills and resources. It is actually quite easy to rob the voice of doom and gloom of its influence. Not only is it easy, but it can be good fun.

Introduce a new character to the house of doom and gloom

Think for a moment of a time when someone said something that upset you. It could be an argument, or a criticism or a parting of the ways. Once you have identified that time, before you experience it again, change their voice to Donald Duck's voice. As you hear that memory you may find the sound of Donald Duck squishing and squashing the words puts a whole new meaning to them. An old Arabic proverb sums it up: *'Better a thousand enemies outside the house than one inside.'* You can now neutralise the enemy within by turning the voice to that of your favourite cartoon character.

It's not very easy to be upset by Donald Duck is it? You may find the incident now raises a smile rather than a frown, or at the very least a wave of confusion or surprise. Try it on those less than helpful family sayings. In your confusion or surprise or even delight you might want to experiment with some other auditory sub-modalities.

Exercise: experimenting with auditory sub-modalities

1 This time, think of a time when you were excited, energised and happy; a time when you were raring to go and were with a group of other people. You may have to start with a visual image but once you have found a memory that inspires you, step into it and experience it as though you were back there, living and breathing that moment all over again. As you become more and more aware of the feelings and sounds, tune in to the voices you hear.

2 As you listen to what you are hearing begin to pay attention to *how* you are hearing it.
   • Is there more than one voice?
   • Whose voices are they?
   • What qualities do the voices have?
   • Are they clear or rasping?
   • Which direction are they coming from?

   • Are they soft or loud?
   • Are they clear or hard to make out?

3 Really get to know *how* you hear what you hear and when you are familiar with the sounds in your mind, switch your attention to your feelings.

4 Get to know how you are feeling when you hear what you hear in your mind. Then begin to play with your auditory sub-modalities.

- What happens to your feelings when you increase the volume of what you hear?
- Return the volume to where it was when you started. Then notice what happens to your feelings when you turn the volume down so the voices are quieter. How would you describe your feelings now?
- Is there a difference to your feelings when the volume is higher, normal and lower?

5 Try some other changes in how you hear what you remember in your mind and pay attention to what happens to your feelings.
- Change the direction of where the voices are coming from.
- If there is more than one voice, make one voice louder or softer. Try making your voice louder or softer than the others.
- Imagine the voices get clearer, or become nasal or rasping.
- Change the voices to your favourite cartoon characters. With each change check out your feelings.

Below is a list of auditory sub-modalities to experiment with. As with values and visuals, what works for you, works for you. You may find changing only one or two sub-modalities will be enough to change how you feel, but only your experimenting with them will tell. Making changes with what you hear in your mind's memory is the only way to discover how your feelings change in response. Once you have discovered the most powerful auditory sub-modalities for you, you can make changes to your state very quickly indeed. Most people want to feel good and would prefer not to have their feeling work against them. Changing how you experience events can help you achieve feeling resourceful for much more of the time.

Find out what is most powerful for you

- Sounds
- Tone
- Direction
- Distance
- Stereo
- Internal/external
- Melody
- Pitch

- Kind of sounds (voice, birds, music)
- Location
- Volume
- Whose voice
- Quality (clear, muffled, nasal)
- Rhythm
- Duration
- Tempo

Once you know how to operate your sound system you can use it to make yourself happier and your life better. Imagine what it would be like if you only heard encouragement and support from your soundbox? How much more could you achieve if you gave yourself advice and guidance in a tone that helped you feel loved and empowered rather than criticised and put down? Your chatterbox and critic could become your best and most loving friend. All you need to do is change the tone or the volume or the accent or the direction or the character.

Mind mischief

There are all sorts of uses you could put your sound box to. You can go further than Donald Duck. After a girls-only workshop, a wonderfully creative and imaginative participant encouraged the rest of the group to hear Sean Connery in their mind whispering sweet, sensual nothings every time they took their clothes off, or got dressed to go out. From the happy smiling faces there was a posse of women who went home happily imagining that famous sexy secret agent telling them how good they looked, how sexy and appealing they were. With Sean saying good things to them their self-esteem was bound to take a boost. It doesn't have to be the delectable Scotsman – whose voice does it for you? Imagine them saying wonderful things to you. You might just enjoy it.

If you are a man, choose someone whose voice you find warm, attractive and sexy. Imagine what a difference it could make having that warm, sensuous, sexy voice encouraging and flattering you. Do you think it might raise your self-worth?

Use your imagination; what else could you do with this new and exciting toolbox? You may want to start neutralising those less than helpful family sayings, change the voice, or the tone, make them louder or softer, change the direction, whatever works. Perhaps you could speed up your voice in your mind when you wanted to get hyped up and excited. This is a great way to motivate yourself to get up and out of bed if you find the lure of 'just another five minutes' too seductive to resist. Not too surprisingly, doing the opposite can have the opposite effect. If you want to relax, calm yourself down then slow down the pace of your chatterbox. If you slow it down enough you may just send yourself to sleep. It is much more effective for dozing off than having pictures and sounds racing around in your head.

Using your physiology to change state

Another ingredient of the recipe for state is in your physiology: how you hold your body, your posture, breathing, tension and so on. If you are depressed you probably drop your shoulders, look down and move slowly. If you are excited you are energised, upright, breathing fast, with your head held up. Both physiology and thinking interact and affect our behaviour, which in turn interacts and affects our state and physiology. Our mind, body and spirit are connected and are all part of the same system. Which is why flying a kite or gazing at the stars can have such an uplifting effect. By changing our posture and looking up we change our state.

Choosing your state

When you are in a resourceful state you can achieve much more. When you are feeling down or are not at your best it can seem that life conspires to bring you down even further. Not true; it is just that when you are down and upset you take things much more personally and seriously. At that moment you only see the dark and the dim. Since no one has ever taught us how we operate, our minds have been running along with very little positive guidance. Our minds are programmed almost like a computer, and how they get programmed is by the experiences, the conditioning, the lessons we have learned on the way.

The great news is that you can now re-programme your mind. If you use the techniques in this chapter you can programme your mind to make the best of every resourceful experience you have had and want to have. Enhance your good memories until they are very strong and powerful for you, until your internal experience is one that is helping you be the best you can be. Diminish those experiences that hold you back. Drain the colour from them and see them so small and insignificant in the distance that they can no longer influence you.

You now have the 'mind magic' handbook that explains how to use the amazing tools and equipment you have in your mind and body. The equipment you have taken for granted is now available to you in lots of new ways. Like any great wondrous tools, they have to be picked up and played with before they are truly fun and effective. So have a good look, enjoy the bright and colourful patterns and dimensions. Get the feel of them, the smooth and the rough, the warm and the cold; luxuriate and savour them. Whatever you do make sure you get to know them intimately, through experimentation and play rather than just by reading about them. You are wholly unique; therefore the way you use your equipment will be unique to you. Form a learning partnership with the ideas and techniques you can use to improve the quality of your life.

Usually the most beautiful and useful tools are the ones that have been tried and tested in the art of creating. When you first pick up the tools they will be strange, different from what you might have used in the past, but as you give them a chance to work for you, when you see what you are creating and building, your confidence and trust in your tools and your abilities will increase.

Summary

By managing your mind you can have access to a wonderful life. You are in a much better position to handle anything that comes your way and make the best of every moment of your life. Your inner experience is only known to you through your sensory systems: what you see, hear, feel, taste and smell. By changing what see, hear and feel you change your inner experience. How you see, feel and hear can make those memories and imaginings strong and powerful or distant and weak. Taking charge of your internal experience gives you choice about how you approach and enjoy your life. Now you have the tools at your disposal, you can have access to positive memories and resourceful states when you need them.

- Your state guides your behaviour and opens possibilities for you.
- You can empower yourself using your imagination and your memory.
- *How* you see, hear and feel things is as important as *what* you see, hear and feel.
- Discovering that *how* works for you means you can make good memories powerful, and negative ones fade away.

Taking charge of your state allows you to take charge of your life.

7 Find the Key to the Best you can Be

Now that 'mind magic' has given you the power to change your inner experience, let's use it to make the best of the resources you have and turn the limitations of the past into learning lessons. Programme your brain with new options, new filters to validate. The old ones have probably been in place for a while, but by making the new ones big, bright and bold you can drown out the old ones until they slowly fade out. When your inner experience is melodious, bright, colourful and vibrates with sparkle and energy it attracts the same in your external world.

Add music and colour to the past

You already have many resources at your disposal, so let's make them as powerful as possible. Start by intensifying your positive memories; go back and juice up those positive experiences until they sizzle and shine. Look back at the timeline exercise in Chapter 1 and all those times you know you were fulfilling your values; start with them. Make those memories big and bright and beautiful and step into them. See what you saw in full, big, bright, magical technicolour. Really make those memories strong and vibrant and warm and melodious for you. Even in the less joyous times there may have been moments of learning, pleasure and positivity. Focus on them, intensify and turn up their volume. Make your past a kaleidoscope of colour and an orchestra of sounds, pleasures and joy. You will feel lighter, more resourceful and more able to deal with the future.

Then ask your unconscious to do the same to all your memories as you sleep. Once you train your unconscious it is perfectly capable of doing it by itself. You can use that process of generalisation to help you multiply the good stuff so that your past motivates, supports and energises you.

Develop a habit

Start developing powerful memories for tomorrow. You may enjoy doing this yourself before you go to sleep. Find something good in the day to juice up. Every day has its little moment of pleasure, even if it is only the sound of a bird in the garden, the aroma of good food or the company of a good friend. Explode it into a riot of colour and sounds and feelings of happiness and joy. Add the smell and taste of good times, and develop a great and resourceful past to help you create a great present and future. Remember that there is only so much that we can pay attention to, so we might as well pay attention to the good stuff.

> When you focus on what is good in your life, your attention and attitude will seek out more.

Instant resources

Start building your resourceful states. Resourceful states are easy to create as you now know, but it takes time and attention to create them. Imagine how wonderful it would be if you could go into any state you wanted: confidence, calmness, acceptance, relaxation, fun, focus, love, passion, joy, just with a touch or a word. That would certainly improve the quality of your life. Now you can. You can build a resource bank of useful states you can conjure up any time you want. There is no excuse now for wishing it could be different. *'I wish I could be that self-assured'*, *'I wish I could get myself motivated'*, *'I wish I could be assertive.'* You may find it easier to recognise these qualities in someone else but you have probably had them at one point in your own life. You have experienced at one point what it is like to be motivated; what it is like to be assertive; what it is like to be self-assured. If you have done it once you can do it again if you choose.

One way to go immediately into a positive resourceful state is to install an anchor. An anchor brings your positive state back automatically without you having to go through the procedures for creating it again and again.

An anchor is an association between a trigger and an immediate response to that trigger. An anchor leads you automatically to a different state. You already have a set of anchors that have occurred without you being aware of them. For example, a loved one smiles at you in that special way and your world becomes a happy and loving place. You hear the screech of tyres and you become alert and responsive. You smell cut grass and you remember a wonderful summer. An old love is brought back when you hear 'your' song on the radio.

An anchor can be the signal for a sequence of states and behaviours. One part of the experience brings up all the other parts. You will probably find if you repeatedly do something, you have given yourself an anchor to get yourself going. Switching on the computer or rolling up your sleeves can act as an anchor for narrowing your focus and concentrating on what you are about to do. If you repeat something often enough or if there is a strong emotional state it gets anchored. And each time you run through the sequence again it gets anchored even more strongly.

> An anchor leads you automatically to a different state.

Physical anchors

You can create an anchor in each sensory system. If someone is smiling and happy and you touch them on the elbow, that will trigger them to feel good when touched in the same way in the future. If someone is laughing uproariously and you slap them on the back, the next time you slap them on the back they will be inclined to be in a fun mood. If you create a state where you are compulsively motivated to do something, and you raise yourself onto your toes (this becomes your anchor) just before you get into action, you will have made the stepping up a vital part of the experience. Next time you want to create the experience you can trigger the anchor, in this case stepping up onto your toes will start the ripple of senses and sub-modalities coming into place to create that powerful, motivated state.

The best way to know it is to experience it. Set an anchor for yourself for motivation. That is a resource we all find useful.

Exercise: setting an anchor

1 Think of a gesture you could physically do that could act as your trigger for being motivated. Make it something you would not trigger by accident. Perhaps clenching your fist, or pressing the tip of your finger and thumb together, or even raising yourself on your toes. Choose a physical action that you can use in the future in public (without being arrested!), and that would not tend to be triggered accidentally. Once you have chosen your trigger for being motivated, relax and anticipate how wonderful it will be when you...

2 Go inside yourself and remember when you were strongly motivated to do something. When you really wanted it so badly, you were almost compelled (even if it was only to eat that chocolate bar). You may want to intensify the strength of your motivation by making the image bigger, turning up the brightness, or amplifying the sounds. You know what works best for you. When you have a strong sense of yourself being motivated, step into that image and experience it.

3 As you step into the picture and the motivation builds and intensifies, do whatever gesture you have chosen for your anchor. If it is stepping up, step up then step forward; if it is a clenched hand, clench your fist and step forward. Continue to experience full technicolor motivation. Breathe it into every cell, every muscle and every part of you. Make sure you are fully associated, right in it and seeing it through your own eyes. Make the experience as vivid, real and present as it was when you first experienced it. Make sure you are giving yourself the anchor as you are going *into* the peak intensity of the experience. You want the build-up, not the let-down. You don't want to be anchoring coming out of the motivated state. This works best when you are just reaching the peak of intensity of being motivated.

4 The next step is to test and see if the anchor works. To make sure you are able to change to a motivated state by firing the anchor you have

installed you have to break state, which means walk around, get back to normal. Forget about it for a moment or two then come back to it.

5 Now it's time to test your anchor to discover if it works. With the same pressure and duration, fire off your anchor. That means set the sequence in motion by repeating the gesture. If it was stepping up, step up. If it was touching your finger and thumb together, do that again. Now pay attention to how you are feeling, what you are seeing and hearing. Check that the experience of being fully motivated comes back.

6 To build the anchor to majestic proportions, repeat the procedure several times until firing your anchor can lead to a state of motivation that is just as strong and compelling as the original experience.

7 When you are happy you have the state of motivation available at your command. Stop and discover other ways to enhance your state.

As well as physical anchors you can develop visual and auditory anchors, and use them to reinforce the physical one. You can develop a visual anchor when you see an image, in your mind or externally, that you have associated with a state. A sound or tone can also trigger that automatic response. Let's really work on building that motivational 'oomph'. By setting a visual anchor, as well a physical one, we are reinforcing and juicing up our ability to motivate ourselves at will.

Exercise: installing

1 Choose a visual image you want to use as an anchor for motivating yourself and go through the steps of the previous exercise. When you are getting to the peak of the state of motivation and are about to fire off your kinaesthetic anchor, think of your visual image at the same time. Your visual anchor is now part of the experience.

2 Break state, think about what you had for breakfast. Come back and test that your visual anchor worked. Think of what it was as you fire your gesture and notice if your state comes back.

Finally, you could give yourself a verbal anchor as well, just to make the state as accessible and strong as you possibly can.

Verbal anchors

1 Give yourself instructions for what you want. You can use a phrase, *'I'm going for it'*, or *'When I say "Yes!" and step up and see myself going for it, I will be completely motivated'*, or you can use a word such as *'motivated'* or *'yes'*. As long as you say it to yourself with feeling and in a tone that would motivate you. Say it with excitement and oomph. You know what will be right for you.

2 Again when you are firing off the other anchors, add your verbal anchor.

3 Break state and test. Fire off all three anchors at once; the gesture, see the image and say what you chose for your verbal anchor. You should be so motivated that you could consider yourself unstoppable.

Remember, the stronger the emotional involvement and repetition the more the power and accessibility of the association between your anchors and your state will strengthen. To strengthen an anchor it is best to practise it, add to it and reinforce it in all systems. However, you can set an anchor in just one system.

Anchoring is a powerful process

A few words of caution here. Anchoring is a powerful process. Make sure you anchor resourceful states only and you are anchoring the same state. Check that the sub-modalities are the same when you set your anchor in each system. Otherwise you will end up anchoring different states and the body gets very confused. Like anything else in life it tends to get easier the more you do it. Some people get astounding results the first time they install an anchor for themselves. With other people it takes a bit more practice.

You are already an expert at installing anchors – your life is full of them. What you are learning now is how to do something consciously and by choice, rather than unconsciously and by accident. The conscious mind is slower than the unconscious but it gets there in the end.

Success states

You will probably have an idea of which states it would be good to have access to at any time. Here are a few suggestions that may not immediately come to mind but can be very useful for helping you achieve a more fulfilling life.

It may be worthwhile cultivating your creative state to come up with other useful states and resources. If you think about it, there are many other states which would add to your ability to shape your life and your happiness.

Curiosity

When you are curious about something you tend to lose your fear of it, especially if it is something new and unknown. Curiosity leads you to explore, to see things from different angles. It opens you up to new possibilities. Remember the curiosity you felt about those presents under the Christmas tree? How would you approach change if you were curious about it rather than apprehensive? How would you approach people if you were curious about them rather than thinking you 'knew' who they were? Try curiosity for yourself.

Safety and security

Often it is the strong sense of security that allows us to take risks and face uncertainty with ease. The sense of safety and security that centres us most is the one that resides inside ourselves. Finding that sense of knowing we are OK allows us to take on the world. Focus on those times you felt safe and secure in your environment and with other people, and make those memories as powerful and enveloping as you can. Even if it was only when we were young, we all had a place where we felt safe and secure.

Satisfaction

One of the most damaging and draining effects on someone's self-esteem is their dissatisfaction with what they have done. Some people seem to lack the ability to find any sort of satisfaction with themselves or their performance. Sometimes this happens because they have not set any standard or criteria to know when they have achieved what they wanted, or they set such unrealistic standards no one could ever meet them. They expect perfection of themselves and focus on the one thing that could have been better.

Most people carry out a post-mortem on their performance; it is helpful for knowing what could be improved and it is also great for congratulating yourself and building a sense of achievement, but not if it leaves you with a permanent sense of 'not good enough'. Learning to be satisfied with what you have done, without it having to be completely perfect in every detail, will bring a lot more happiness and a lot less self-doubt into your life. Be satisfied with the things you do have rather than dissatisfied with the things you don't have.

Satisfaction allows you to enjoy the decisions and actions you have taken. It is worth cultivating. Even if it is only satisfaction with a good meal, or something you have bought, you will probably find satisfaction has been present at some time in your life. If it has been present once, it can be again.

Letting go

Hanging on to things that have been finished or completed can cause pain and depression. Some people finish a project and keep on refining and re-editing it. It is nearly there but not quite. Someone gets promotion but still keeps on 'helping' the person in their old job. A relationship breaks up, but years later one of the partners is still mourning, hoping to rekindle it or plotting revenge. Hanging on may be because someone's reluctant to move on to something new, or they find the process of 'doing' is more enticing than the completion of the project. Either way it keeps you stuck. When you let go you make room for new possibilities. You can move on with the benefit of all the memories, learnings and experiences that will be useful to you in the future.

Commitment

A very useful state that is almost crucial to getting what you want, is commitment. Commitment is what keeps you going long after enthusiasm and motivation have worn off. That is what gets you up in the morning, keeps you at it and keeps you trying different things until you get what you want. If you give up you can never succeed.

Thomas Edison kept himself in a resourceful state of commitment to his idea and eventually it paid off. With drive and determination, Edison continued to try different ways to get his light bulb to fulfil the potential he had visualised for it. Even after 999 attempts he was still proclaiming, *'I've just found another substance that does not conduct electricity.'* Rather than give up or be depressed, he chose to view each outcome as more information to work with rather than as a failure. Every time he discovered a material that did not work he tried something different. His ability to think of the results this way opened up the possibility for him to succeed. If he had thought of it as a failure he might never have been motivated enough to persevere and get the outcome he desired. He was committed enough to keep on going until finally he got the results he wanted.

In her book *Total Confidence*, Philippa Davies provides several more wonderful examples from the world of publishing on the power of commitment:

- It took 23 submissions before James Joyce's *Dubliners* was accepted by a publisher.
- Before it sold seven million copies in the USA, Richard Bach's *Jonathan Livingston Seagull* was returned by 18 publishers.
- Twenty-one publishers turned down *M.A.S.H.* by Richard Hooker before it was finally published and became a massive best seller.
- Richard Adams' *Watership Down* was rejected 72 times before being accepted.

All those authors who continued to submit their manuscripts eventually got what they wanted. If they had not continued to be committed to themselves and the outcome they wanted, they might have stopped trying.

How many other great manuscripts have never been published because the authors lacked commitment. They started their project but never finished it. They may have had great ideas, they may have had talent, they may have created a literary masterpiece that we will never know about because they gave up. In their heads maybe five attempts were enough for them to brand themselves or their work as failure. For others it may have been 25 rejection slips.

How many rejections or different outcomes than you had planned classify as failure in your mind: one, five, ten, one hundred, one thousand? What is your magic number for giving up? How did you decide on that number? How many people have the commitment of Richard Adams? Next time you think of giving up, think of Richard and the rabbits of *Watership Down*. Every time you switch on a light, you might like to be reminded of Thomas Edison and his 1000 attempts. What a great anchor for reminding you of the power of commitment and perseverance.

Learning from others

If you can't remember a time you were committed, think of someone you know or have read about who has a strong sense of commitment. You can benefit from other people's experience and excellence directly by *modelling* the successful elements or steps of what they do well. This goes deeper than copying, more than actually doing what they do, but also adopting their process for thinking and feeling as they do. *What* and *how* they think and feel are essential parts of the distinct strategies and elements that make up 'how to'.

Imagine how Edison produced the results he did. What would he have been saying to himself? How would he have been behaving? What about Richard Adams: what are the beliefs he must have had about himself and his work to continue to be committed to see it published? What kinds of conversations were going on in his head? How was he seeing himself and his work? What kinds of mental strategies were these men using until they got the results they wanted?

Borrowing resources

There are probably people around you whom you could model and from whom you could borrow talents or strategies for achieving their outcomes. Watch how they approach the world. Ask them what they believe. You can learn enough to adopt what they do and bring their qualities into your life.

Identify the resource you would like, then choose someone you know who has the qualities you are after. It should be someone who you have seen and heard in action. Keep in mind it is only the specific resources, the beliefs that are pertinent, the mental strategies for achieving what they do. You do not want to be a poor imitation of anyone else. Unfortunately many people fail to differentiate between the skills or resources a person has and the person themselves. Be selective – only go for the resource you want.

Exercise: borrowing resources

1 First identify the resources you need, then identify someone who has them.

2 Imagine that person is there in front of you, doing what you want to be able to do.

3 When you have a strong image of that person, step into it. Get into 'their skin' as much as possible. Adopt their posture, their mannerisms, their breathing. Become them as fully as you can, doing what it is you want to 'borrow' from them.

4 Notice what kind of things you are saying, what you are doing, what beliefs, what strategies you employ when you become that other person. Experience as fully as you can what it is like to be this person who has the ability to do what you desire. Pay attention to the differences between what they do to achieve their outcome and what you do.

5 Make sure you are comfortable adopting the beliefs and values that may be in place for them to achieve their outcome.

6 Take note of the sub-modalities of this state. How and what do you see? How and what do you hear? How and what do you feel when you are 'in their skin' achieving what you want? Are there any smells or tastes that are part of the experience?

7 Step out of their skin and come back to being yourself again. Notice if you were surprised? Did you learn something unexpected?

Often this exercise brings us in touch with some of the stuff hidden in the unconscious broom cupboard. We often know a lot more about other's strategies than we imagine. Once you have done this exercise you may find you have other questions to ask of your model. Most people are very flattered to know they have been picked out as someone who is excellent at what they do.

Once you have had a chance to think about it, discover if you are happy with your new resources. You may want to go back and refine them. When you are happy you have everything you need for yourself, anchor this state for future use. Taking this time to review gives you a chance to explore if you are at ease with everything that goes with these new resources.

Case study

Teresa wanted to be able to have the resource of what she called *'putting herself forward'*. She identified an acquaintance Paula, who was very skilled in selling herself. She was extremely successful in developing new opportunities and getting people to help her. To Teresa she seemed the idea model to 'borrow' the resource from. When Teresa stepped into her role model's skin she became very uncomfortable. Her experience of her role model was of *'almost being a two-year old again. It was all me, me, me! I want, I want, I want! Complete tunnel vision for herself with no sensitivity to anyone else's feelings.'* For Teresa the price of the resource from this role model was too high. The perceived strategy did not fit in with Teresa's values and she was able to find the resource from another model whose strategies and state she was happy with. So check out how comfortable you are before setting an anchor.

Recognising your own resources

Often, the biggest problem people have is in recognising when they have the resources they want. Abby could not think of an instance when she had been committed to anything. In fact, she thought she gave up too easily at anything she tried. Yet Abby had just finished telling us about getting up every morning at 6 a.m. to take her dogs for a walk before she left for work. No matter the weather, no matter how she felt, Abby was committed to the welfare and wellbeing of her animals, just as she was committed to the welfare of her family. There was no question about it – yet she did not recognise it. Abby probably had more experience of the power of commitment than anyone else there in the room but she could not see it for herself.

Similarly she could not identify a time when she felt confident, yet once again when she spoke about her children and her animals she radiated confidence and assurance. Abby might not have had the confidence for public speaking or for entering a party by herself but she was very sure of her ability to care for those who were important to her. When Abby changed the sub-modalities of public speaking to the same as being 'a good caretaker of my family' she realised she felt relaxed and at ease and very sure of herself. If you have something that works well in one area of your life you can definitely use it somewhere else.

> Sometimes your resources are in the most unexpected places.

Rehearse it

One way Abby used her state of confidence was for doing a presentation at work. Several times she imagined herself running through the presentation with confidence and ease. She saw herself being centred and assured, and her audience responding well to her. She heard her voice fluent, steady and calm and she felt focused and relaxed. After three or four rehearsals in her imagination she was raring to go. The apprehension she had felt about giving her first presentation had gone. She had rehearsed it so many times in her head it felt like old hat to her. Her mental rehearsal gave her the opportunity to plan ahead, anticipate any questions and be prepared. You may find the same technique applies for you. If you are going to do something new or something you are unsure or apprehensive about, rehearse it a few times in the appropriate state and discover how much easier it makes the real thing.

Taking others into account

You can also use this process to take into account other people around you, how they and you will respond to any changes you want to make. Any changes will affect other parts of your behaviour, your life and your relationships. Use rehearsal to check before you make a change that it really is what you want. You may want confidence to be successful at work and get a promotion, but you may also be worried about the amount of work you have to do and how it will affect your family. Look and listen out for the effects of that change. Is there any part of you that objects? You may need to add more resources or adjust your goals. You may want to add other resources, such as balance and assertiveness, so you can say 'no' to work.

Remember, you are a system and your relationships and life are all part of a system – any change in one part will have repercussions on the rest. Check for the effects of what you do both for yourself and the other important people in your life.

Unlock the magic of your mind to predict a great future

Many of these principles draw on the power of creative visualisation. You may have rejected the idea of it in scepticism, yet this is what you have used when you created your disaster movies. Instead, you could use it to create new beliefs and new filters. Your beliefs act as perceptual filters so that you only notice what validates them. If you start to create strong experiences that invalidate your old beliefs and support your new ones, very soon your inner experience will start to filter your new beliefs. They will become part of your reality.

Take your states and imagine how you will be in the future when you have those resources fully present with you. Turn up their sub-modalities until they are magnificent and compelling, and rehearse your future so often it becomes a memory. Have you ever woken from a dream and been unsure if it was real or not? The only way you know if something is real or not is how you code it in your sub-modalities. Find out how you code your sub-modalities for a past resourceful memory and code your future in the same way. That way it becomes inevitable. Try the same process for changing your beliefs.

Change your beliefs

One of the most valuable resources you can have is empowering beliefs. One way to challenge limiting beliefs is to simply re-code them in a more appropriate way. You will already have a way of knowing what you believe in and what you don't. Otherwise you would have to consider and remake the decision of whether you believed it or not every time something came up. Your mind is too well organized for that. Your beliefs operate your perception filters. What you believe will have its own distinct sub-modalities. Check it out for yourself. In Chapter 5 you made a list of the beliefs that have limited you in the past and a list of five beliefs that can help you reach your ideal future. How did you know what you believed and didn't believe? We are back to your processes of thinking: your five senses.

Exercise: re-coding limiting beliefs

For the first part of this exercise, think about something you believe in. Make it something simple that there is no doubt about. Perhaps something like *'I need to eat to live'*, or *'I should wear clothes to go to work'* (if, of course, you do believe it). Make sure it is something that you are completely and utterly sure about, like the need for air. Pay attention to the sub-modalities of what you believe

1 Now how do you see it?
   - Is it a movie or a still?
   - Is it in colour or black and white?
   - Where is it?
   - How close is it?
   - How big is it?
   - Does it have a border, is it panoramic?
   - What other qualities do you see?

2 How do you hear it?
   - Can you hear any sounds?
   - Is it voices or something else?
   - Whose voice?
   - Are they inside your head or outside?
   - In mono or in stereo?
   - Pay attention to the direction, tone, loudness and any other qualities you notice.
   - How do you feel?
   - Do you notice anything going on in your body?
   - Where is it?
   - What would you call that feeling?

- Be aware of temperature, lightness, density, size and any other qualities.

Once you know how you are aware of the sub-modalities that mean you believe something, compare it with how you code something you doubt. Again, make it something simple. Something you doubt like being able to fly without wings, or you running a mile in 30 seconds. Take note of the sub-modalities of doubt.

Compare the sub-modalities of both. Notice the location of each, the size, colour and so on. Then check out the sounds, voices, rhythm, tone of each one. Pay attention to the feeling that goes with both. What are the differences? Take note of them, we will use them to change those limiting beliefs you identified in Chapter 5.

Look at your list of limiting beliefs and the list of empowering beliefs that would be more useful to you now. Choose one of each to work with.

1 Identify your limiting belief.

2 Ask yourself what do you believe about that belief. Step back from the belief and ask how useful it is to you now.

3 As you compare the sub-modalities of belief and doubt, notice how they differ. Identify the sub-modalities that distinguish them.

4 Change the sub-modalities of belief to doubt one at a time, until you identify the one that most powerfully alters the belief.

5 Identify your new and positive belief. State what it is in positive terms and as though it is already with you. *'I can cope with any situation easily and with confidence.' 'I can learn quickly and thoroughly.'*

6 Check the ecology of this new belief. Does any part of you object to having it?

7 Change the sub-modalities of limiting belief to doubt.

8 Switch the sub-modalities back and forth. As you get used to doing it, do it faster and faster. Do this repeatedly. Go quickly back and forth from belief to doubt until it gets easier to do. Keep at it until you get disoriented, dizzy or confused. When you are at that point it is time to put in the new belief.

9   Turn all the sub-modalities down on limiting beliefs until you can't see, hear or feel any of its limiting content. Replace with the content of your new empowering belief and turn up all of the sub-modalities again. Switch this to belief then doubt several times, back and forth several times. Stop when it is in belief.

10   Adjust the sub-modalities until it is compelling and irresistible. Breathe it in, let it sink in, consider what this looks like, sounds like, feels like. Imagine what it is like in the future when you are operating out of this new and supportive belief.

11   Break state. Think about breakfast and then think about the subject of the limiting belief. What happens?

You may want to do this with all your limiting beliefs, and install new ones instead. Then reinforce and support them by what you tell yourself.

Turning your chatterbox into your best ally

Your internal dialogue could make a big difference in confirming your new filters and beliefs. If you have a toxic voice in your head you are creating a toxic life. Consider the findings of two researchers, Clark and Teasdale (1985), who looked at the effects of mood on memory. They brought two research groups together to have a different musical experience. One group was played happy, uplifting music (*Coppélia* by Delibes), which put them in a good mood; and the other group got *Russia under the Mongolian Yoke*, a musical extract by Prokofiev from a Russian film. This depressing music was played at half speed just to make it even more sorrowful. Not surprisingly the ones who listened to *Coppélia*, the bright, happy music, felt happy and the other people who got landed with the miserable music reflected the tone of the music in their feelings and their thoughts. The ones who felt down because of the music remembered more bad times in their life and were less confident in their abilities to complete a relatively simple task successfully than those who heard the happy music. If that happens when listening to music can you imagine the effect of toxic people in your life, and one of those toxic people could be yourself.

Often our internal dialogue can chatter away in the background without us being aware of the effect it is having. The whole time it can be beavering away, nagging, whispering or screaming at us. A constant running commentary about ourselves, other people, the world. For some people their critical voice can mentally torture and abuse them, for others their inner voices are a source of support and encouragement.

Consider the difference when you are about to try something new. If you have a scathing voice saying to you, *'you'll never do it, you're no good at anything'*, how encouraged would you be compared with hearing an excited and loving voice that shouted, *'Yes, go on, you can do it!'* How much more encouraged would you be if you turned down the volume on those old unsupportive messages and found instead the voice of belief and encouragement?

> If your internal dialogue is so taken up with reprogramming your new beliefs and filters it drowns out those old messages.

Reprogramme your chatterbox. Replace those negative, worn-out noises with more constructive beliefs, ideas and concepts. Make your new inner chatter strong, positive statements in the present tense as though you had them right now. You are programming your attention and attitude to make this your reality. Base them on the new beliefs and the new ways of thinking you are putting in place. If you have had a critic in residence before, it may be worthwhile sending yourself new messages of acceptance, love and appreciation.

When you are at ease with yourself you can accomplish so much more and you can give so much more to other people when you are no longer defending yourself from a hostile inner world. Experiment with your auditory sub-modalities, try them in different tones, from different directions, different volumes, rhythms and so forth. Find the voice that means business, the voice of *'definitely so, no doubt about it'* and try them with that; or find the voice of pleasure and laughter and experiment with that one. You will know which one works best for you when you try it.

Here are a few suggestions from an infinite number of possibilities. Try out a few of your own. You will instinctively know what is right for you.

- I am worthy of acceptance and love.
- I can handle anything that comes my way.
- I am confident and a winner.

- I am happy and successful.
- I am fit and healthy.
- I deserve the best that life has to offer.
- I am interesting and can do anything.

Keep at them. Eventually you will want to replace them as they become redundant.

So far we have concentrated on building up your positive experiences so that you have much better access to all the resources at your disposal. The next useful step is to take the power away from those negative experiences that may be limiting you. Before you do that it is useful to have a very resourceful state at hand that you can use to lift yourself up if you get bogged down in an unresourceful state.

Exercise: unlock the magic of your mind to create a state of excellence

1   Chose a physical, visual and verbal anchor you can fire for bringing back the resourceful state of excellence.

2   Identify an excellent state. Name a state that you would like to have as a resource, a state that has you at your best and in the flow.

3   Imagine a circle on the floor. As you think of the circle on the floor imagine it big enough for you to step into.

4   Flood the circle with a colour that symbolises the resource. Notice how the circle transforms, begin to notice the qualities of the circle in terms of depth of colour, size, density, temperature, smell and so on.

5   As you watch the circle in front of you, think of a time or imagine when you had that excellent state. You may be able to find the qualities within yourself or borrow them from someone you know who has them. Make it as real as possible. Fully experience how you feel, what you say to yourself, what you see and how you hold your body when you possess these abilities and qualities. Breathe them in until they are a part of every muscle, every cell, every movement. Anchor this state.

6   Imagine yourself in the circle, bathed in the colour, possessing all the qualities and abilities you want. Hear what you say to yourself, see what you look like and notice what you now feel.

7   Fire your anchor and step into the circle of excellence. Step into that picture of yourself and as you associate into those thoughts, memories, awareness and feeling. See what you see, hear what you hear when you have all these abilities fully present and available. Know that these qualities are part of you and that they will continue to grow and increase with each day.

8   As you stand in the circle experiencing the resources that are part of you, imagine how you will use them in the future as they increase and grow. Think of the situations that will arise and see hear and feel yourself performing exactly as you would like to in these special situations…

9   Knowing that these resources are part of you and can be called on any time in the future, step out of the circle.

10   Break your state – think of what you had for breakfast. Test by firing your anchors that your excellence state is strong enough for you. If you need to juice it up, go back and recycle through the exercise again until it is powerful enough.

You may want to use the same process for establishing other resourceful states

Diminish your limitations

If you think back to the timeline exercise in Chapter 1, you might have found it was the negative experiences that came up first so they could be stronger in your memory. It may be worthwhile choosing a couple of these disempowering memories and taking the sting out of them. You can still have the learnings from those experiences, but when the images are so small, and dim and distant, their power is diminished. If you get stuck in a negative memory, fire your anchor for your state of excellence to help you be at your best to deal with it.

- As you bring the negative memory to mind, make sure you are watching yourself in the movie or slide.
- Push it away from you, make it smaller, watch it fade away into the distance.

- As it moves away and becomes smaller, watch the colour drain out.
- Move it so far away it becomes a dot on the horizon.
- As the image shrinks do the same with the sounds.
- Lower the volume of the sounds and voices, drain their energy down until they are slow and lethargic.
- Let the feelings lose their shape and power. Let them mist over and fade away.

Do this with a few negative memories. Start with mildly unpleasant ones; your unconscious will soon get the message and start to do it by itself.

This too will pass

Resources can be anything. Just knowing 'this too will pass' is enough sometimes to help someone going through a difficult time. Most people have good times and bad times in their life. It can vary from person to person and time to time, but most of us have a life that goes up and down. There are joyous, melodious periods and other spells when the music of life becomes a dull, disheartening drone.

When everything is going well in your life you tend to look back and remember mainly the good times. You have full access to all of your re-sources, the joys and pleasures in your life. Your past and future look rosy and bright. In contrast, it becomes more difficult to get in touch with those positive times when you are upset and worrying. Your life begins to sound like a constant whine, a whine that drowns out any possibility of a better time now or in the future. When we are stuck in the middle of the darkness, just the knowledge that light will come again can be a lifeline, a valuable resource to have.

Record your resources

Often you can lose sight of the resources you have, especially when you are down and need them most. At this time it is great to have a written record of them that you can use to jog your memory. Take the time and be as creative and inventive as you or anyone else can be and make a list of all the resources you have; the role models, the teachers (in whatever form), friends and family who have contributed to you, your education,

your finances, your time, your strengths, your skills, your resourceful states, your energy, your inspirational books, the music and beauty around you
…
The more you search the more you will find.

Summary

The potential for creating powerful and supportive states and beliefs for yourself is limited only by your imagination. Each of us has had great moments in our life which can empower us time after time. Every day we can add to them if we focus on the joy rather than the irritation in our life. We all know people who are their own worst enemy. They spend their time griping and complaining about the little things that are lacking rather than the great bounty they have. These are the people who claim they live in the real world, but it is only a real world in their mind. They live in a dim, dark, world of their own making. Be a rebel, add colour to yours. The more colour you add to your present and your past the more you will create in your future.

An anchor can bring your resourceful state back automatically. We create anchors by associating part of an experience to one of our five senses – these signal the sequence of states or behaviours. Learning from others and borrowing their resources can be another effective way of getting the results you want. Reprogramme your inner experience by changing your beliefs and your chatterbox.

- Anchors are shortcuts to a resourceful state and can be purposefully created.
- Anchors can herald a particular sequence of states or behaviours.
- If you have a resource in one area of your life, use it in others too.
- If you are unable to harvest particular resources, borrow them from others.
- Rehearse your empowering state and behaviour in your head and visualise yourself succeeding.
- You can reprogramme your beliefs and chatterbox to support you.
- Record your resources for when you need reminding of how much you have.

Take the power out of those limitation of the past.

8 Go for It!

To create the life you want and live it to the full means making those changes and adjustments that will get you where you want to be – you have to do something different to achieve something different. If you do what you have always done you will get what you've always had. Packy Ease did not have much luck as a boxer, so he did something different. He changed his name and his job and found a great deal more success as Bob Hope. He got the successful outcome he wanted, but he had to take action to make it happen.

Plan for your fantastic future

It is now time to put together the action plan for your fantastic future. You are starting to make it real. You know what your values are, you know what you want in your future and you have some useful tools to support you. Now you can take action to bring your ideal day into your life. Unless you make a plan and put it into action, your ideal future may remain a colourful motivator and a great possibility – but that is all. By breaking it down into step-by-step achievable outcomes or steps along the way you multiply your chances of success.

You can set and focus on short-term and long-term goals to get there. Every time you achieve a goal it keeps you motivated, on track and focused. If you didn't set and achieve milestones along the way you would never have the pleasure of patting yourself on the back for your achievements. The more you achieve the more you find you can achieve as confidence builds on itself. Each step, each goal you set and fulfil will encourage you to keep going. Each pat on the back, each congratulation, reinforces the beliefs that you can and will create the kind of life you want and deserve. Each achievement becomes a resource for the future. Let's get specific and set some goals for the year ahead.

Step 1 – select a goal

What do you want? Remember to say what you *want*, not what you *don't want!* Ensure it is a solution that will take you towards a great future rather than backing away from present problems. Be positive and specific in what you want. Anne set herself three goals – to become fit and healthy, to have a great relationship with her family and to start her own business (Chapter 2).

Declare what you want

Instead of saying, 'I don't want to be a fat slob', ask yourself what you want instead. 'I want to be slim and fit', 'I want a great relationship with my family', will help you achieve a lot more than 'I don't want to feel like a stranger in my own home.'

> Make sure you give yourself a direction so that all your efforts and energy, conscious and unconscious, are pulling in the same way – forward.

Step 2 – break it down into manageable size steps and stages

Break the main goal into smaller outcomes so you can attain them easily and motivate yourself to continue achieving them. Being slim and fit is a great outcome for you, but it may seem overwhelming. It could put you off. Breaking it down into easily achievable and sustainable steps makes it easier to accomplish and gives you a map to follow if you go off course. Not *'I will lose two stones in two months'*, but rather *'I will change to healthy eating habits. I will lose two pounds a week. Every day I will go for a 30-minute brisk walk and twice a week I will go to the gym.'* That is much easier to keep to and return to if you go off track.

Be specific

Anne's *'great relationship with my family'* is a wonderful goal, but it is a bit abstract. Breaking it into smaller specific actions that would bring about the final goal made it easier for Anne to achieve. She broke it down by asking herself, *'What actions would bring me a great relationship with my family?'* What she came up with was, *'I will be more playful with my family. I will sit down and talk to my children every day. Every day I will give them a hug and I'll compliment them and talk to them about something personal, rather than homework, cleaning their room or what they have done wrong. I will book a babysitter and going out with my partner once a week and I will arrange a romantic week-end away for the two of us and a family holiday this year.'* Every time she accomplished one of her steps she felt good about herself and her achievements. Each step motivated her on to the next one.

When you make it easy to accomplish your goal and you know exactly what to do you have more chance of making it happen. Break it into goals that motivate you: that may mean breaking it down even more or making them bigger and more of a challenge – whatever works for you.

Step 3 – know when you have achieved your goal

Give yourself a way of knowing that you've got what you wanted. That way you will recognise your success when it comes. Sometimes this step is helpful for realising the goal you stated may not actually bring you what you thought it would. If Anne wanted to be slim and fit to save her marriage, she might find that achieving slimness and fitness did not bring her the real goal she wanted; saving her marriage. Other steps and resources might be necessary for that.

Ask yourself:

- What will I see, hear and feel when I have achieved my goal?
- How will I know when I have reached my goal?
- What evidence do I require to know I have achieved my outcome?
- What will I be doing or not doing when I am 'living my goal'?

How would Anne know she had achieved her goal of being slim and fit?
Every week on the way she would *see* herself ticking off the achieved weight on her diary.

✓ Her clothes would *feel* looser on her.
✓ She would *hear* herself less breathless as exercising became easier and more enjoyable.
✓ After two months she would *look* at the scales and they would read two stones less than when she first set the goal.
✓ She would *fit* into her grey suit again.
✓ She would *hear* other people complimenting her on looking slim and healthy.

That was her evidence for having reached her goal. What about a great relationship with her family? Her evidence would be:

✓ *Seeing* herself laughing, playing and enjoying herself with them.
✓ *Hearing* herself being honest and open about her feelings with her husband and children.
✓ A warm glowing *feeling* in her stomach.

One way or another you will have evidence, but what about something more abstract like 'safe and secure', or 'centred?' How would Anne know she had achieved her goal of playfulness or self-confidence? We asked:

- Will you see yourself behaving differently?
- Will you see others behaving in a certain way with you?
- Would you be doing something you had never done before or doing it in a new way?
- Will your pictures be bigger, more colourful, clearer or brighter?
- Will you be speaking to yourself in a different tone, saying different things, slower or quicker, hearing different things?

- Will your voice be deeper, louder, have a new rhythm or timbre; will you be using different words?
- Will you feel different?
- Could there be a change in your posture, breathing, the way you hold your shoulders?
- Could the evidence be a sweet smell, or a delicious taste, or a warm bubbly feeling?

Anne's evidence would be personal to her. Everyone has their own way of knowing.

> Recognise when you have achieved what you set out to achieve.

Step 4 – define the context

Decide when, where and with whom you want your outcome. You may want to be more assertive – but all the time, in every situation? You may want to imagine when you particularly want to be assertive. You may find there are plenty of occasions where you don't want to be assertive. As well as finding out when you want it, it can be useful to know when you don't want the behaviour. The goal of being relaxed and confident may not be appropriate when you are contemplating trying something new and unknown, or are about to be attacked. There are times when a bit of anxiety and stress can be useful for preparing us and alerting us to what is required of us.

Check out your outcome by imagining having it in real-life situations. Ask yourself:

- Would I want it in every situation, every relationship, all the time?
- How long do I want to do or get this? (You may want something different on holiday, for instance.)
- Where will the change take me?
- Where would this be useful?
- Where would it hold me back?

Anne wanted playfulness, but in the right place and at the right time. Being playful with her children would be great most of the time, but there were would be occasions where she would want to be serious with them. And playfulness may not be the most appropriate resource for her to take to work with her. Anne wanted self-confidence to help her start her own business. The first step was having the confidence to share some of her discoveries about the change curve with Ralph, her boss. Getting specific allowed her to identify an essential first step for her.

> Defining a context helps you get specific and focus on where and when you need your resources most.

Step 5 – recognise if it is in your power to obtain

Make sure the goal you set is something you can control or influence. A realistic goal might be to go out and play your best in a competition, but an unproductive goal is winning the competition. You cannot control other people's performance, only your own. That type of goal only sets you up for failure and disappointment. You can't depend on other people changing or on winning the lottery. Recognise that while there are some things you can completely control, other things you can only influence and some things you have no sway over at all. So when you set your goal make sure it is something you can initiate and keep going, and that means taking full responsibility for yourself and your actions without blaming other people or circumstances.

> When you try to control other people, you set yourself up for failure.

Anne's goal of taking care of herself and getting to her ideal weight is totally within her control – so is starting her own business. Having a great relationship with her family she could strongly influence, but she cannot completely control because   relationships are a system. Her actions can influence the system greatly, but others also have a choice. As long as she keeps that in mind, she could go a long way to initiating it and bringing it about. Go for it as fully as you can. Set an outcome that is obtainable and under your reasonable control. If it's not, you may be wasting your time and energy that could be better directed to achieving what you can influence. Ask yourself:

- To what degree can I own this outcome, both in initiating it and then bringing it about?
- What will I do to achieve this goal?
- Could anything get in the way of me achieving my goal?
- Does it depend on me alone or on someone else?
- *What do I need from other people to obtain this?*

Step 6 – is it healthy and wholesome for me?

Check it out: is this something you really want or is it something you 'should' want? Before you put the time and energy into achieving this goal, how do you know it is the right goal for you?

Often, one of the most valuable resources that people have is time. When Abby was doing the magic wand exercise the thing she would wish for most was two extra days a week to get everything fitted in. Before you take on too much more, think about what you might have to give up to do it. Spend your time doing those things you value or that help you achieve your outcomes. Too often the important things can get neglected for the mundane, the drudgery. If this is happening to you, check out your direction. How much of what you are doing is compatible with your values? Molly spent most of her time keeping her home spotless, but the family she was doing it for were never comfortable in their own home, and she was so busy cleaning she had no time to spend with them. How realistic are your standards? Are you a perfectionist? Is it appropriate in that context? Perhaps that perfectionism could be a valuable resource to use elsewhere.

Use your values as a guide

When you keep in mind your values, you can get down to what is important as soon as you can. You don't need to spend time procrastinating. If it does not feel as though it fits in with your long-term future, if it may cause you internal conflict, then perhaps you should put it to one side. Ask yourself:

- Does it fulfil my values?
- Who do I have to be to obtain this?
- Is it in tune with my identity and life purpose?
- *Is it a win-win for me?*
- For others in my life?
- What will be the future consequences of my goal on myself and others?
- *What could I lose by achieving this outcome?*
- What further goal does it take me towards?
- And for what purpose?

It can be useful to recognise *how* you know that you want it. Does the picture pulsate and draw you forward? Is there a voice that says, *'yes that's it!'* Is there an irresistibly warm and excited feeling in your solar plexus? Could there be an enticing smell or taste that lets you know this is what you want? How do you identify it?

> If you keep in mind your values there is no need to spend time procrastinating and deciding what to do.

Taking others into account

What about other people you care about? This great new promotion you have put all your energy and attention into getting, may mean your relationships suffer because you are not around. How will achieving your goals affect them? Before you make the changes, take into account the effects on important others in your life. If you upset the present balance, can your renegotiate a different one that suits them too? Otherwise you may find they go on to make their own changes, which may not include you.

Anne decided to take at least a year to start her new business: she recognised that it would be best for all the family if she waited until her partner had finished studying and her children were a bit older. She decided to put the year to good use by planning and researching her new company.

Step 7 – acknowledge the pay-off of the present

The odds are that you are getting some kind of benefit for what is happening at the moment, otherwise you would not be doing it. Before you set your outcome, consider the pay-off or benefits of what you have now. Unless you can hold on to the benefits of what you have now, or find a way to compensate for them, you may end up stopping yourself. If you want to keep the benefits but cannot find a way of incorporating the present benefits (not the behaviour) into your future outcome you may want to rethink the cost of your goal.

Be honest with yourself. If you are doing or not doing something at the moment, no matter how destructive or painful, you are getting a pay-off from it. There is some kind of benefit in it for you. If you go to bed at night like Anne and promise yourself; *'Tomorrow I'm going to do something different: I'm going to get fit, I'm going to get out and exercise and eat food that is healthy'*, and then tomorrow you disappoint yourself, somewhere there is a benefit for you. You may firmly want to get back into the suit you wore last year, but that bar of chocolate or pint of lager is just too tempting. Getting back into the suit might take time. You would have to wait for the pleasure of that, and the pull of immediate gratification can be more enticing. This is another good reason to set small, achievable instant gratification steps when setting your goals.

You too may want to start your own business, but that means taking risks and sticking your head out, and it's much safer keeping it down. Joan wanted to say *'no'* to people but didn't want to be thought of as selfish or be disapproved of. Even though you might desperately want to do or not do something you are getting a big pay-off from preserving the status quo. You have to be getting something out of it, otherwise you wouldn't do it. You might want to change your boring job but your pay-off for staying stuck is staying in your comfort zone. You may want to get healthy but staying in bed is more pleasurable at that moment. You may be unhappy in a relationship but you don't want to be on your own or lose out financially.

Remember those needs we talked about in Chapter 2, the need for security, control and self-expression, love and affection, belonging? If you look deep enough you will probably find your pay-off satisfies one of these needs. If you can't find your pay-off you are not looking or listening attentively enough.

Pay-offs are powerful. They can also be very healthy and supportive. Sometimes you can trade them. If you eat well, maintain an enjoyable exercise programme and take care of yourself, your pay-off will generally be vitality and good health. Trade the pay-off of instant gratification for a bigger, brighter picture of that vitality and good health. If you plan your future using your values and take responsibility for bringing it about, your pay-off will be happiness and fulfilment. That is a pay-off worth having.

So, as a pattern, it is always worth asking of every action – *'What is my pay-off?'* and *'What am I getting out of this?'* Unless we take them into account and find another way to satisfy them we will end up sabotaging ourselves. We may end up suffering from internal conflict as we have competing pay-offs.

Consider the desire of Phil (Chapter 2) to explore new things, to live his life full-out, but at the same time wanting to feel safe and secure. To resolve his conflict and make the changes he wanted he found a way to feel safe and secure within himself while exploring and taking sensible risks. And that meant finding the resources within himself to do so.

Consider what you are getting out of your present situation or state before you make a change. If you don't recognise what you are getting at the moment and don't find a way to fulfil it with other resources, you may sabotage your outcome or be very dissatisfied when you get it. Ask yourself:

- What do I gain by my present situation?
- What would I lose if it changed?
- What will I get once I have reached my outcome?
- What effect will it have on my life?
- What would not happen if I achieved this goal?
- What would happen if I didn't achieve my goal?
- What would not happen if I didn't achieve it?

Step 8 – identify the resources you need to make it happen

To an extent this checks the realism of your goal. *'I want to become Prime Minister'* may be a great goal, but if you are 60 and have never been in politics it is highly unlikely to happen. However, there may be opportunities for those prime ministerial qualities to be put to use elsewhere, on the parish council or local council, for instance. Charities are often looking for people to be involved as volunteers and trustees.

Often people have more resources that they realise. Anne had set herself quite a large goal in starting her own business. There were many unknowns about running her own company. When she thought about it there were lots of practical things to consider, including information-gathering about how to start her business, and where to get financing; but for most of these she thought she could get help through books and small business advisers and courses. When she looked at her list she realised that she already had them herself at one point, or knew how and where to get them. Getting access to each resource became another goal on the way to starting her own business.

Anne's resource list:

✓ Confidence
✓ Motivation
✓ Focus
✓ Organisation
✓ Decision-making
✓ Creativity
✓ Following things through
✓ Assertiveness
✓ Persistence and stamina
✓ Balance between business and family
✓ Self-discipline
✓ Strategic planning
✓ Assertiveness
✓ Identifying mentors and role models and asking for help
✓ Getting down to work.

If you are happy with your answers then the only thing that is stopping you is you!

Often people have more resources that they realise. They do not lack abilities, skills or resources – they lack the belief in themselves and the way to get in touch with their resources.

Go for it!

When you set a goal you leave no room for confusion or doubt. You know where you are going and how to get there. When your goals are in tune with your values, you are heading in the right direction. Just follow the eight steps to achieving your goals and you are well on the way to creating the life you want!

Exercise: using the eight-steps strategy

Let's get specific and set some goals for the year ahead. Look back at your ideal days from the timeline exercise. Choose a goal that will help you create those ideal days. These goals can be steps to achieving what you want ultimately for your long-term future, or they may be short-term goals you want right now. Go through the eight-step process to ensure the outcome is worth having and that you have considered every angle.

- Step 1 – Select a goal: state it in the positive, go for what you want and not what you want to avoid.
- Step 2 – Break it down into manageable steps and stages. Make it big or small enough for you to be motivated and able to achieve. That keeps you on track and you get the instant gratification and confidence when you do it.
- Step 3 – Know when you have achieved your goal – what will you see, hear and feel when you have achieved it? Give yourself criteria for success, otherwise you could be chasing what you already have!
- Step 4 – Define the context; when, where and with whom and under what circumstances do you want this to happen? When do you not want it to happen?
- Step 5 – Recognise whether or not it is in your power to obtain. Can you initiate this goal and then keep it going? How much does it

depend on other people? If you need others' co-operation, is it something they would want to co-operate with?

- Step 6 – Is it healthy and wholesome for you? Have you considered the outcome and consequences for yourself and other people?
- Step 7 – Acknowledging the pay-off of the present – what are you getting out of the present situation? Are you safe in your comfort zone, do you get to feel good about yourself or connected to other people by your current situation? How can your new outcome fulfil your benefit?
- Step 8 – Identify the resources you need to make it happen. Do you know who has them or where to get them? Has there been a time in the past when you have had them? Is it physically possible for you?

If you have followed these steps you should know what you want and how to get it. Put it in your diary, on your wall calendar, print out your goals and tick them when you achieve them. Keep them in sight – then do it. Get in touch with your passion for life and go for it!

Everyone deserves to have the life they want and live it to the full. Many more people than ever before are designing their ideal lives and developing themselves to be the very best they can be. Join forces with them. When you are with others who are living by their values, together you will energise and help each other grow. When you live your life to the full you become a role model and resource for others. Your influence goes well beyond you; it goes on for generations to come. Remember the only failure in life is not living it to the full!

Summary

- Follow the eight-steps strategy to ensure your outcome or goals are everything you expect them to be.
- Select a goal and go for what you want.
- Make your goal big enough or small enough for you to be motivated and able to achieve it.
- Give yourself criteria for achieving the outcome.
- Decide when, where and with whom and under what circumstances you want this to happen.
- Make sure your outcome is something you can control or greatly influence.

- Consider the outcome for yourself and other people.
- Take into account what you are getting from the present situation.
- Identify the resources you need to make it happen.
- If the answer is yes – then go for it!

Good luck!

Index